Autosanctity in the Age of
Hegemonospheres

Spirituality and Society

Autosanctity in the Age of Hegemonospheres

GRAHAM JOSEPH HILL

Eagna Publishing • Sydney, Australia

AUTOSANCTITY IN THE AGE OF HEGEMONOSPHERES

Published by: Eagna Publishing (Sydney, Australia)
eagnapublishing@icloud.com
Cover and interior design: Graham Joseph Hill
www.grahamjosephhill.com

paperback isbn: 978-1-7644455-5-9
ebook isbn: 978-1-7644455-6-6
version number: 2026-01-20

NATIONAL LIBRARY OF AUSTRALIA

A catalogue record for this book is available from the National Library of Australia

Contents

Introduction: The Sacred Self in a Fractured World

Something strange has happened to the sacred.

We were told it would disappear. As science advanced and societies modernized, as education spread and superstition retreated, the sacred would evaporate: a morning mist burned off by the rising sun of reason. Churches would empty. Temples would become museums. The gods would take their place alongside Zeus and Odin in the cabinet of human curiosities. We would be left with a disenchanted world, cool and procedural, where disagreements were settled by evidence and compromise, where moral fervor gave way to tolerance, where people agreed to disagree and got on with their lives.

That isn't what happened.

The sacred didn't disappear. It relocated. The transcendent God who once grounded meaning, morality, and identity has been replaced by the immanent self, which now bears the full weight of those functions. The self has become holy ground. To trespass on it is to commit sacrilege. We live in an age of autosanctity: the sacralization of self in a supposedly secular time.

This explains the puzzle of our moment. Secularization was supposed to cool things down, to drain the heat from our conflicts, to make disagreement manageable. The opposite has occurred. Moral fervor has intensified. Heresy-hunting is rampant. Excommunication is swift and thorough. The exile isn't from a church but from professional networks, social circles, and the warmth of public approval. The language of the denunciations is therapeutic ("harmful," "unsafe," "toxic"), but the

1

grammar is religious. Heretics are identified. The community is protected from contamination. The sacred must be defended.

"We're tired because the self was never meant to be a god, and we've made it one."

We're tired because the self was never meant to be a god, and we've made it one. The burden is too heavy. The temple is too small. The worshiper and the worshiped are the same, and this identity is exhausting. There's no sabbath for the autosanct self. Construction never ceases. Identity is never complete, never secure, never safe from challenge or obsolescence. The self must be continually maintained, updated, defended, and performed. Rest would mean stagnation. Silence would mean invisibility. The self can't simply be; it must perpetually become.

The Fracturing

Meanwhile, the world itself is fracturing.

The architecture of international relations that emerged from the ashes of the Second World War, refined through the Cold War and triumphantly declared universal after 1991, is crumbling. In its place, we're witnessing the emergence of hegemonospheres: distinct zones of influence where major powers shape the political, economic, and informational realities of their client states. The United States, China, and Russia each anchor their own gravitational field, pulling neighboring nations into orbits of dependency, allegiance, and shared fate. The rules-based order hasn't vanished, but it no longer commands universal assent. Sovereignty has become conditional. Borders are contested. Power determines outcomes.

The connection between these developments isn't accidental. When the self becomes sacred, loyalty becomes tribal. When identity must be defended, difference becomes a threat. When recognition is the oxygen of existence, those who withhold it become enemies. The culture wars that rage within Western societies echo the geopolitical fractures between them. The temperature keeps rising because everyone is burning the same fuel: the defense of what has been made holy.

And the technologies that promise to connect us have, instead, amplified fragmentation. The digital environment serves as an anti-desert: filling every silence, enabling endless escape from self-confrontation, monetizing our attention while starving our capacity for depth. We're the most connected generation in human history and among the most exhausted. We carry in our pockets devices of staggering power, portals to all human knowledge, instruments of instant communication across continents, and we use them, often, to perform our identities for audiences we'll never meet.

What This Book Offers

This book offers a diagnosis and an invitation.

The diagnosis is autosanctity: the cultural condition in which the self has become the primary locus of sacred meaning. Understanding this condition helps explain the intensity of our conflicts, the exhaustion that pervades contemporary life, and the strange new shapes that ancient human needs have taken in a supposedly secular age. The need for ultimacy doesn't disappear when God is removed from the frame. It attaches to something else. In our case, it's attached to the self.

The invitation is to lay down the burden. The self doesn't have to be its own ground. It can be received, known, and named from beyond itself. It can rest in an identity it did not construct. The self that learns to say "I'm not my own" will find, at last, the rest it could never give itself.

These reflections were first shared with readers of my Substack, *Spirituality and Society with Hilly*, and they're gathered here as a single conversation: an attempt to understand our moment and to point toward another way of being human within it. The writing emerges from the Christian tradition, which has its own resources for diagnosing autosanctity (the self, in this account, is a creature that can't bear the weight of ultimacy) and its own alternative (an identity received as gift, grounded in divine love, freed from the exhausting labor of self-construction). But the diagnosis applies across traditions, and the

3

invitation extends to anyone who senses that something has gone wrong with the way we're living.

The Shape of the Book

The book is divided into four parts.

The first part diagnoses the sacred self. It defines autosanctity, traces its roots in the therapeutic turn and the immanent frame, and examines how digital technology both feeds and fragments the self it claims to serve. The desert fathers and mothers who fled to the wilderness in the early centuries of Christianity understood something we've forgotten: that we become what we attend to, and that attention itself must be trained, protected, and sometimes radically withdrawn from the noise of the world to be restored.

The second part examines autosanctity in public life: in the emerging hegemonospheres that are reorganizing global power, in the celebrity culture that elevates and destroys public figures, in the housing crisis that reveals how material conditions shape spiritual possibility, and in the moral complexity that resists tribal certainty. These chapters press against the temptation to make autosanctity a weapon against one's political opponents. The condition appears across the spectrum, in progressive and conservative forms, in religious and secular expressions. The log in one's own eye remains the first order of business.

The third part confronts what breaks autosanctity open: suffering that can't be explained and technology that challenges human uniqueness. The book of Job offers no easy answers to the problem of innocent suffering, and this refusal is itself a gift. The doctrine of divine retribution (the belief that the righteous prosper and the wicked suffer) is one more attempt to make the self the center: my suffering must mean something about me. Job refuses this logic and points toward a God who enters human pain without explaining it away. Meanwhile, artificial intelligence raises the question of human distinctiveness with new urgency. If machines can replicate the capacities we once thought made us special, where does dignity rest? The Christian answer points beyond function to

4

relationship: the self is made for communion with God, and this vocation remains when all the capacities fail.

The fourth part offers the theological alternative to autosanctity. The Incarnation announces that God has entered creation, that the sacred isn't found by escaping the material world but by recognizing that God has joined himself to it permanently and irrevocably. Christmas is the declaration that hope has taken flesh, that an identity is being offered to the exhausted self, that the cosmos has a future that the self did not construct and can't destroy. The final chapter, written in response to tragedy, shows what it looks like when the sacred self gives way to solidarity with suffering neighbors: grief, presence, the refusal to let fear have the last word, and the commitment to be one people across every divide.

The Invitation

Autosanctity in the Age of Hegemonospheres isn't a manual or manifesto. It's an attempt to see our moment clearly and to point toward what lies beyond it. The essays gathered here were written in different seasons, in response to different occasions, yet they circle the same questions: What has happened to the sacred? Why are we so exhausted? Where can the weary self find rest?

The answers I offer emerge from Christian faith, from the conviction that the self is a creature made for relationship with God and neighbor, that identity is a gift before it's an achievement, that the one who loses his life will find it. These convictions aren't arguments to be won but possibilities to be inhabited. They require communities that embody them, practices that form them, and the strange grace that enables people to step off the treadmill of self-construction.

The invitation is simple, though never easy: to receive an identity you did not make. To rest in a worth that doesn't depend on performance. To lay down the terrible freedom of self-creation and take up the lighter burden of creaturehood.

"The invitation that stands against autosanctity is the invitation to be held."

5

The sacred self is weary. It's been performing for so long. The audience is never satisfied. The construction is never complete. There may be another way.

The invitation that stands against autosanctity is the invitation to be held. The collapse is into arms that are waiting. Giving up is the beginning of receiving. The letting go is how one discovers that one was held all along.

The question isn't whether the sacred self can sustain itself. It can't. The question is whether we'll notice before we break.

And the question, finally, is whether there's a word from beyond ourselves, a voice that speaks over the noise of our endless self-construction, offering what we can't give ourselves: rest, identity, belonging, home.

There is.

That's what this book is about.

PART I: DIAGNOSING THE SACRED SELF

Part I: Diagnosing the Sacred Self opens with the foundational "Autosanctity" chapter defining the core concept, followed by "Tech Sabbath" showing how digital technology both feeds and fragments the sacred self.

1. Autosanctity: The Sacralization of Self in a Supposedly Secular Age

In 2015, a Nobel Prize-winning biochemist named Tim Hunt attended a conference in South Korea. During a toast at a luncheon, he made an ill-judged attempt at self-deprecating humor about women in laboratories. Within hours, his remarks had been tweeted, condemned, and amplified worldwide. Within days, he had resigned from his honorary professorship at University College London, from the Royal Society's awards committee, and from the European Research Council's science committee. A forty-year career in cell biology, including the Nobel-winning discovery of cyclins, effectively ended over a clumsy joke at lunch.[1]

The speed and totality of the response startled observers. Hunt's remarks were foolish, the kind of generational gaffe that might once have prompted eyerolls, a rebuke, perhaps a forced apology. Instead, the reaction carried a particular heat. The demand was not simply that he acknowledge error or learn from criticism. The demand was for professional annihilation, social exile, the comprehensive dismantling of his public standing. The language of the denunciations was therapeutic ("harmful," "unsafe"), but the grammar was religious. Heresy had been identified. The heretic had been cast out. The community had been protected from contamination.

---

[1] Louise Mensch wrote extensively about Tim Hunt on her blog Unfashionista/louisemensch.wordpress.com. See also Jonathan Foreman's account here: https://www.commentary.org/articles/jonathan-foreman/the-timothy-hunt-witch-hunt/

This intensity is the puzzle. Secularization was supposed to cool things down. As religious authority receded, disagreements would become procedural, amenable to compromise, settled by evidence and argument rather than anathema. Pluralism would reign. People would agree to disagree. The opposite has occurred. Moral fervor has intensified. Heresy-hunting is rampant. Excommunication is swift and thorough. The exile isn't from a church but from professional networks, social circles, and the warmth of public approval.

The explanation isn't that religion has simply returned, or that "wokeness" is a religion in disguise, though that framing captures something real. The explanation is that the West has not abandoned the sacred. It's relocated the sacred. The transcendent God who once grounded meaning, morality, and identity has been replaced by the immanent self, which now bears the full weight of those functions. The self has become holy ground. To trespass on it is to commit sacrilege.

I want to name this condition "autosanctity," from the Greek *auto* (self) and the Latin *sanctitas* (holiness, inviolability). Its behavioral expression is "the sanctimony of self": the righteous certainty that accompanies the defense of one's identity, and the moral revulsion directed at anyone who questions it. Understanding autosanctity helps explain both the intensity of our cultural conflicts and the exhaustion that pervades contemporary life. We're tired because the self was never meant to be a god, and we've made it one.

Defining Autosanctity

Autosanctity is the cultural condition in which the self has become the primary locus of sacred meaning. The West has relocated the sacred from the transcendent God to the immanent self, which now bears the full weight of grounding meaning, morality, and identity.

"Autosanctity, from the Greek auto (self) and the Latin sanctitas (holiness), names a cultural condition in which the self has become sacred ground. The West has relocated the sacred to the self. The transcendent God who once grounded meaning, morality, and identity has been replaced by the immanent self, which now bears the

9

full weight of those functions. This explains why contemporary cultural conflicts carry such religious intensity: to question someone's identity is no longer mere disagreement but desecration."

Autosanctity isn't narcissism, though narcissism flourishes within it. Narcissism is a personality trait or disorder; autosanctity is a cultural condition with institutional expressions, shared assumptions, and liturgical forms. A humble person can be shaped by autosanctity. A selfish person can resist it. The question isn't whether individuals are self-absorbed but whether the culture treats the self as the ultimate source and arbiter of meaning.

If autosanctity names the cultural condition, "the sanctimony of self" names its characteristic tone: the righteous certainty that accompanies the defense of one's identity, and the moral revulsion directed at anyone who questions it. Sanctimony originally described hypocritical or performative holiness. Here, it captures the performative dimension of identity in an age when authenticity must be publicly demonstrated and socially validated to feel real. The sanctimony of self is what autosanctity looks like in practice: the speech, the posture, the readiness to condemn.

Under autosanctity, the self plays a dual role. It's both the priest who performs the sacred rituals and the god to whom those rituals are directed. The self constructs, expresses, and demands recognition of its identity. The self determines what is true for the self, what is good for the self, and what obligations the self will accept. Any external authority that would impose identity, judge identity, or constrain self-expression becomes suspect, an oppressive force to be resisted.

The philosopher Charles Taylor has described our era as an "age of authenticity" in which the highest good is being true to yourself.[2] He has also described the "immanent frame," the shared assumption that this material world is all there is, that transcendence is unavailable or

---

[2] Charles Taylor, *A Secular Age* (Cambridge: Harvard University Press, 2007), 473–504. Taylor's concept of the "age of authenticity" describes a cultural condition in which the highest good is being true to oneself and one's particular way of being human.

illusory.[3] Autosanctity names what happens when these two features combine with the ineradicable human need for the sacred. The need for ultimacy doesn't disappear when God is removed from the frame. It attaches to something else. In our case, it's attached to the self.

This helps explain why sexuality has become such a fierce battleground, a phenomenon Stephen Alpine has insightfully labeled the "sexular" dimension of contemporary secularism.[4] Sexuality is where self-expression, embodiment, and social recognition converge most intensely. Sexual identity feels profound, essential, and defining. To deny or question someone's sexual self-understanding is experienced as an attack on their very being. But sexuality is only one theater of autosanctity. The same dynamics appear in consumption choices, political affiliations, dietary practices, career identities, and wellness regimens. Wherever the self is expressed and recognition is sought, autosanctity is at work.

The Liturgies of Autosanctity

Every sacred order develops liturgies: repeated practices that enact and reinforce its vision of reality. Autosanctity is no exception. Its liturgies are so pervasive that they've become invisible, part of the background hum of contemporary life.

The most recognizable liturgy is public confession. Individuals share their identities, traumas, struggles, and journeys on social media platforms designed to elicit and reward such disclosure. The architecture of these platforms encourages confessional performance: the prompt "What's on your mind?" invites introspection; the metrics of likes and shares quantify the reception of one's testimony; the feed ensures an audience. These aren't private journals but public altars.

---

[3] Taylor, *A Secular Age*, 539–93. The "immanent frame" refers to the constructed social space that frames our lives entirely within a natural order, without reference to transcendence.
[4] Stephen McAlpine, "A Sexular Age," stephenmcalpine.com, July 11, 2015. McAlpine coined the term "sexularism" to describe secularism's particular focus on sexual ethics as a primary battleground.

The confessions follow recognizable patterns. There's the identity testimony: "I'm coming out as..." There's the trauma testimony: "I've never shared this before, but..." There's the growth testimony: "I used to believe X, but I've done the work, and now I understand..." Each form establishes the confessor's authenticity. Each invites recognition, affirmation, and the solidarity of others who share similar experiences.

Within autosanctity, suffering confers authority. Those who have experienced something possess truths unavailable to those who haven't. This inverts older epistemologies in which detachment and objectivity were cognitive virtues. Now, proximity to pain is the credential. "As a survivor of..." or "Speaking as someone who has lived..." become epistemic trump cards. The logic makes sense within the framework: if the self is sacred, then the self's experiences are revelatory. Those who have not had certain experiences must defer to those who have.

Tending the sacred self requires specialists. Therapists, life coaches, wellness practitioners, and self-help authors occupy the cultural space once held by priests and pastors.[5] This isn't a criticism of therapy as a clinical practice, which addresses genuine suffering with genuine skill. It's an observation about how therapeutic concepts have migrated far beyond clinical contexts to become the moral vocabulary of everyday life. "Boundaries," "trauma," "toxic," "healing," "self-care," "triggers," and "safe spaces" now function as the primary terms in which ordinary people interpret their experiences and make moral judgments.

The shift can be seen in a simple substitution. Where an earlier generation might have asked, "Is this good?" we now ask, "Is this healthy for me?" The first question assumes external moral standards against which actions can be measured. The second question locates the standard within the self's psychological experience. Health replaces virtue. The therapeutic practitioner replaces the confessor. The DSM replaces the catechism.

---

[5] The concept of therapeutic culture as a successor to religious culture is developed in Philip Rieff, *The Triumph of the Therapeutic: Uses of Faith after Freud* (New York: Harper & Row, 1966).

"Where an earlier generation might have asked, 'Is this good?' we now ask, 'Is this healthy for me?' Health replaces virtue. The therapeutic practitioner replaces the confessor. The Diagnostic and Statistical Manual of Mental Disorders (DSM) replaces the catechism."

Every sacred order also identifies heretics and administers discipline. Autosanctity is fierce on this point. Those who transgress its core commitments face swift social consequences: public denunciation, professional sanction, relational exile. The charge is rarely framed as "You're wrong" or "You've made an error in reasoning." The charge is "You're harmful," "You're unsafe," "You're denying my existence." These formulations make perfect sense within the logic of autosanctity. If the self is sacred, then questioning someone's identity claims isn't a disagreement but a desecration. It's violence against the holy.

This explains the puzzle of intolerance within a supposedly tolerant framework. Autosanctity is tolerant of diverse identities, the more identities, the more occasions for sacred self-expression. But it's fiercely intolerant of challenges to the framework itself. You may be anything you wish. You may not question whether someone else's self-understanding is accurate, healthy, or grounded in reality. That question is blasphemy.

Consent and the Minimalist Ethics of Autosanctity

When the self becomes sovereign, ethics faces a problem. Sovereign selves will come into conflict. Their self-expressions will collide. Some principle is needed to adjudicate. But the principle can't come from outside the selves, because external authority is precisely what autosanctity has rejected. The solution has been consent. The only legitimate constraint on one sacred self is the agreement of other sacred selves.

Consent-based ethics has genuine achievements to its credit. It names coercion clearly. It identifies assault and exploitation. It insists that persons may not be used against their will. These are real moral gains, and cultures that lacked robust consent norms permitted terrible abuses.

The problem isn't that consent matters. The problem is that consent has become the sole criterion, the only moral concept with any remaining purchase.

This creates strange gaps in moral reasoning. Autosanct culture can be exquisitely sensitive to subtle forms of coercion, power imbalance, and manufactured consent. The discourse around sexual ethics, for instance, has developed sophisticated analyses of how intoxication, authority differentials, or social pressure can compromise consent. This attentiveness is often valuable. But the same culture struggles to articulate why a fully consensual arrangement might still be degrading, exploitative, or corrosive to human flourishing. If both parties agree, what grounds remain for critique?

The category of "bad for you" has become almost unspeakable. To suggest that someone's freely chosen path is self-destructive sounds paternalistic, judgmental, and a violation of their sacred autonomy. The only recognized harm is harm to which one did not consent. Self-harm, by definition, is consented to and, therefore, immune from moral evaluation by others. At most, one might gently inquire whether the person has really thought it through, whether they're aware of the consequences, and whether they might benefit from talking to someone. But the possibility that an external standard might reveal the choice as genuinely wrong, regardless of consent, has been foreclosed.

This explains a peculiar asymmetry in contemporary moral attention. Microaggressions, subtle slights, and inadvertent offenses generate intense concern because they're experienced as violations of the sacred self without its consent. Meanwhile, consensual arrangements that older moral traditions would have recognized as degrading pass without comment. The disparity isn't hypocrisy. It's the logical outworking of a framework in which consent is the only remaining moral criterion.

Autosanctity Across the Political and Ideological Spectrum

Autosanctity isn't the property of one political tribe. It manifests across the spectrum, though in different registers and with different emphases.

Recognizing this is essential to understanding the phenomenon accurately, and to avoiding the temptation to use the concept as a weapon against one's political opponents.

Progressive autosanctity centers on identity and recognition. The sacred self here is often the marginalized self, the self that has been denied recognition by oppressive structures and dominant groups. The demand is that institutions, cultures, and individuals validate identities that have historically been suppressed, mocked, or rendered invisible. The multiplication of identity categories reflects this logic: if the self is sacred, its particularities deserve ever-finer articulation. To subsume distinct identities under generic labels is a form of erasure.

"The culture wars are, in part, a conflict between rival autosanctities, each accusing the other of violating what is holy. The temperature keeps rising because both sides are burning the same fuel."

The language of safety has expanded dramatically within this framework. Physical safety was the original referent, but the concept now encompasses psychological safety, emotional safety, and freedom from discomfort or distress. This expansion makes sense if the self is sacred and inviolable: anything that wounds the self, including words and ideas, constitutes a kind of violence. Safetyism, as Greg Lukianoff and Jonathan Haidt have called it, is the institutional expression of progressive autosanctity.[6]

Conservative autosanctity centers on liberty and choice. The sacred self here is the autonomous self, the self that won't be told what to do by government, experts, or collective pressure. Individual choice, whether in markets, consumption, lifestyle, or belief, is treated as inviolable. Resistance to external claims becomes a matter of principle, regardless of whether those claims might be reasonable or beneficial.

---

[6] Greg Lukianoff and Jonathan Haidt, *The Coddling of the American Mind: How Good Intentions and Bad Ideas Are Setting Up a Generation for Failure* (New York: Penguin, 2018), 23–34. Lukianoff and Haidt coined the term "safetyism" to describe the culture of prioritizing emotional safety over other practical and moral concerns.

The rhetoric of "freedom" and "rights" dominates this formation, but the underlying grammar is autosanct. The self is the ultimate authority. Any imposition on the self is suspect. "Don't tread on me" functions as a theological statement: the self is sacred ground, and trespassers will be met with righteous fury. This explains the intensity of resistance to public health measures, collective obligations, or appeals to expertise. The issue isn't usually the specific policy but the affront to sovereign selfhood that any external demand represents.

What unites these formations is more fundamental than what divides them. Both assume that the self is ultimate. Both treat external authority with suspicion. Both generate intense moral energy in defense of their vision of sacred selfhood. The culture wars are, in part, a conflict between rival autosanctities, each accusing the other of violating what is holy. The progressive sees the conservative as denying recognition to sacred identities. The conservative sees the progressive as imposing constraints on sacred autonomy. Neither sees that they share the same deep grammar.

This mutual blindness explains why dialogue across the divide is so difficult. Each side can perceive the other's autosanctity with clarity while remaining oblivious to its own. Each experiences the other as desecrating the sacred and responds with the fury appropriate to blasphemy. Compromise feels like betrayal, because the sacred can't be negotiated. The temperature keeps rising because both sides are burning the same fuel.

The Exhaustion of the Sacred Self

The deepest problem with autosanctity isn't that it produces cultural conflict, though it does. The deepest problem is that the self can't bear the weight that has been placed upon it. The self was not designed for ultimacy. When it's forced to be its own ground, its own meaning, its own justification, it cracks under the pressure.[7]

Consider the burden of infinite choice. In an autosanct culture, every decision becomes existentially freighted. What you eat, what you wear, what you watch, whom you befriend, how you spend your time: each choice expresses and constructs the sacred self. There's no neutral ground, no realm of mere preference or habit. Everything signifies. Everything is identity. The self is always on stage, always performing, always subject to evaluation.

"There's no sabbath for the autosanct self. Construction never ceases. Identity is never complete, never secure, never safe from challenge or obsolescence."

Authenticity, under these conditions, isn't something one simply possesses. It must be achieved and displayed. The authentic self isn't the self that exists quietly, unobserved. The authentic self requires an audience, recognition, and validation. Social media provides this audience, but the provision is double-edged. The metrics of engagement become measures of authentic success. The self that isn't seen, liked, shared, and affirmed begins to doubt its own reality.

There's no sabbath for the autosanct self. Construction never ceases. Identity is never complete, never secure, never safe from challenge or obsolescence. The self must be continually maintained, updated, and defended. Rest would mean stagnation. Silence would mean invisibility. The self can't simply be; it must perpetually become.

The mental health crisis among young people isn't incidental to this condition. Rates of anxiety, depression, and self-harm have risen dramatically, particularly among adolescents and young adults. Multiple factors contribute, but autosanctity is among them. When the self bears ultimate weight, when identity must be constructed rather than received, when recognition is the oxygen of existence, and when that recognition is mediated through platforms designed to maximize engagement

---

[7] The observation that human flourishing has become its own end, rather than a means to a greater goal such as the glory of God, is developed in James K.A. Smith, *How (Not) to Be Secular: Reading Charles Taylor* (Grand Rapids: Eerdmans, 2014), 20–22.

through emotional provocation, psychological fragility follows. The autosanct self is a self that can't rest, and rest is essential to health.

The irony of self-care is instructive. The term emerged to name practices of attending to one's own well-being: rest, nourishment, boundaries, withdrawal from excessive demands. But self-care has become another obligation, another domain of performance, another way the self must labor on its own behalf. The exhausted self is told to care for itself, which requires energy the exhausted self doesn't have, which produces guilt and shame for failing at self-care, which deepens the exhaustion. The solution has become part of the problem.

Consumer capitalism thrives in this environment. The sacred self requires expression, and expression requires stuff: products, services, experiences, aesthetics. The market offers an infinite number of options for self-construction. You can curate your identity through what you buy, display, and consume. But the relief is temporary. The self's hunger for validation is bottomless, and every purchase eventually proves insufficient. The market profits from the cycle: generate the felt need for self-expression, provide temporary satisfaction, allow dissatisfaction to build, offer new products to address the dissatisfaction, repeat.

The self that must be everything to itself ends up with nothing solid to stand on. The ground keeps shifting because the self keeps shifting. Identity becomes liquid, anxious, perpetually under construction. The freedom that was promised, freedom from all external constraints, turns out to be a new kind of bondage: bondage to the endless task of self-creation.

The Christian Diagnosis

Christianity offers a particular diagnosis of why autosanctity fails. The self, in the Christian account, is a creature. It did not make itself. It doesn't sustain itself. It isn't its own ground or goal. The self is designed to receive its identity from beyond itself: from God, from community, from the givenness of embodied existence, from the call to love and serve. When the self tries to be its own foundation, it's attempting something for which it was not made.

This reframing transforms the meaning of limitation. Autosanctity experiences limits as obstacles to authentic self-expression. The body's constraints, the obligations one did not choose, the expectations of others, the moral law: all appear as impositions on the sovereign self. Christianity sees these differently. Embodiment isn't a prison but a gift, the condition of creaturehood that makes love and action possible. Unchosen obligations aren't oppressions but the very fabric of a life embedded in relationships. Limitation isn't the enemy of flourishing, but its context.

There is, in this vision, a liberation that comes from being told who you are. Autosanctity assumes that any external claim on identity is violence. But what if certain external claims are relief? What if the exhausted self, weary of construction, longs to hear a word from beyond itself? "You're my beloved." "You're forgiven." "You're called." These aren't impositions but gifts. They provide what the self can't provide for itself: a ground that doesn't shift, a worth that doesn't depend on performance, an identity that's received rather than achieved.

Human dignity, in the Christian account, doesn't rest on the self's capacity for expression or choice.[8] It rests on bearing the image of God. This is a more stable foundation. The infant who can't yet express anything, the person with profound cognitive disability who can't construct an identity, the dying person who has lost the capacity for self-determination: all possess dignity, because dignity isn't an achievement of the self but a gift from beyond the self. Autosanctity struggles to secure this kind of dignity. If worth depends on authentic self-expression, what worth belongs to those who can't perform authenticity?

But the Christian diagnosis must be self-implicating. Christians have practiced their own versions of autosanctity, and any critique that

---

[8] The argument that contemporary Western moral categories remain parasitic on Christian foundations, even in their secular expressions, is developed in Tom Holland, *Dominion: How the Christian Revolution Remade the World* (New York: Basic, 2019).

fails to acknowledge this is merely a weapon wielded against outsiders. The sacralization of political alignment, in which partisan identity becomes functionally ultimate. The treatment of cultural preferences as doctrinal essentials, in which particular styles of worship, dress, or social organization become markers of authentic faith. The tribal identities that divide the church, in which being a certain kind of Christian matters more than being united to Christ. These are autosanctities, and they flourish within communities that would reject the label.

The gospel isn't a tribal possession. It's a word that addresses all human beings in their common creaturehood, their common brokenness, and their common need. When Christians use theological language to sanctify their own preferences, or when they adopt the culture-war posture of defending their sacred selves against threatening outsiders, they've surrendered to the very dynamic they claim to diagnose. The log in one's own eye remains the first order of business.

Possibilities for Repair

If autosanctity names a genuine cultural pathology, what would healing look like? The question is easier to pose than to answer. Autosanctity isn't a policy problem with a policy solution. It's a spiritual condition, a disordered orientation of the soul, and its remedy lies at that same depth.

The beginning of repair is the recovery of givenness. The self isn't infinitely plastic. It arrives in a body with particular capacities and constraints. It's born into a family, a community, a history it did not choose. It inhabits a world with structures and limits that precede its preferences. Learning to receive these givens as gifts, rather than experiencing them as impositions on authentic self-expression, is the first movement away from autosanctity. The self that can say "I did not make myself, and I'm glad" has taken a step toward freedom.

Communities of mutual obligation offer an alternative to the isolated, performing self. These are relationships in which members are bound to one another, not merely affirmed by one another. Obligations are unchosen. Belonging isn't conditional on self-expression. The community has a life and purpose beyond the aggregation of individual identities. Such communities are increasingly rare. They require patience, sacrifice, and the willingness to be shaped by something beyond one's preferences. They're also the context in which selves can rest, can be known rather than seen, can fail and be forgiven rather than canceled.

Practices that decenter the self are therapeutic in the oldest sense. Worship directs attention toward God. Service directs attention toward the neighbor. Manual labor directs attention toward the task. Silence interrupts the internal monologue of self-construction. Attentiveness to the natural world reminds the self of its smallness and its participation in something vast and given. These aren't techniques for self-improvement, which would only reinforce autosanctity. They're ways of loosening the self's grip on itself, of allowing the self to forget itself in devotion to something beyond itself.

A different account of freedom is possible. Autosanctity defines freedom as the absence of external constraint: freedom from. But there's another meaning of freedom: freedom for. Freedom as the capacity to love, to give oneself, to be bound in relationships of mutual care. This freedom isn't diminished by commitment but constituted by it. The person who can make and keep promises, who can sacrifice for others, who can subordinate immediate desire to long-term faithfulness, is more free, not less. Autosanctity can't see this, because it can only see constraint as loss. But the self that's freed from the tyranny of its own impulses is a self that has found a larger life.

These aren't solutions in the programmatic sense. They're gestures toward another way of being, another possibility for human life. They require communities that embody them, traditions that transmit them, and the strange grace that enables people to step off the treadmill of self-construction. They can't be implemented by policy or technique. They can only be lived, imperfectly, by those who have glimpsed an alternative and are drawn toward it.

The Self That Rests

The self that makes itself a god will eventually discover the misery of its divinity. The burden is too heavy. The temple is too small. The worshiper and the worshiped are the same, and this identity is exhausting.

The invitation that stands against autosanctity is the invitation to be held. The self doesn't have to hold itself together. It can be received, known, and named from beyond itself. It can rest in an identity it did not construct. It can lay down the terrible freedom of self-creation and take up the lighter burden of creaturehood.

This isn't a strategy. It's closer to a collapse, a giving up, a letting go. But the collapse is into arms that are waiting. Giving up is the beginning of receiving. The letting go is how one discovers that one was held all along.

The sacred self is weary. It's been performing for so long. The audience is never satisfied. The construction is never complete. Perhaps there's another way. Maybe the self that learns to say "I'm not my own" will find, at last, the rest it could never give itself.

"The self that learns to say 'I'm not my own' will find, at last, the rest it could never give itself."

2. Tech Sabbath: Recovering the Desert in the Digital Age

There's a hum beneath everything. You've grown so accustomed to it that you no longer hear it, the way a person living near a highway eventually stops noticing the traffic. It's the sound of perpetual connection: the buzz of notifications, the soft glow of screens in darkened rooms, the endless scroll of information that never quite satisfies and never quite stops. We wake to it. We fall asleep to it. We reach for it in moments of boredom, in moments of anxiety, in moments of silence that we've learned to fear.

"We're the most connected generation in human history and among the most exhausted."

This is the texture of contemporary existence. We're the most connected generation in human history and among the most exhausted. We've access to more information than ancient scholars could have dreamed of possessing, yet wisdom seems to recede the faster we chase it. We carry in our pockets devices of staggering power, portals to all human knowledge, instruments of instant communication across continents, and we use them, often, to watch strangers dance for fifteen seconds at a time.

Something has gone wrong. We sense it in our bones, in the frayed edges of our attention, in the strange emptiness that follows hours of scrolling, in the way we feel simultaneously overstimulated and undernourished. We're drowning in content and starving for meaning.

The ancient monks who fled to the Egyptian desert in the third and fourth centuries couldn't have imagined our world. They knew

23

nothing of algorithms or smartphones, of social media or streaming services. Yet they understood something about the human soul that we've largely forgotten: that we become what we attend to, and that attention itself must be trained, protected, and sometimes radically withdrawn from the noise of the world to be restored.

They called it *anachoresis*, withdrawal. We might call it logging off.

The Desert as Spiritual Geography

In the early centuries of the Christian movement, something remarkable happened. As the faith moved from persecuted minority to imperial religion, as bishops gained political power and churches grew comfortable, a countermovement emerged. Thousands of men and women left the cities of Alexandria, Rome, and Antioch and walked into the wilderness. They sought caves and abandoned tombs, crude huts and rocky hermitages. They became the Desert Fathers and Mothers, the *abbas* and *ammas* whose sayings and practices would shape Christian spirituality for millennia.

Why the desert?

The desert was, first of all, a place of emptiness. It offered nothing to distract: no marketplaces, no theaters, no dinner parties, no endless social obligations. In the stripped-down landscape of sand and stone, these seekers encountered themselves and, in that encounter, encountered God. The desert was a furnace that burned away illusion, a silence that exposed every inner voice clamoring for attention.

"You can't heal what you can't see. You can't offer to God what you refuse to acknowledge."

But the desert was also a place of confrontation. The monks spoke freely of the demons they battled there, the demon of acedia (spiritual listlessness), the demon of vainglory, the demon of lust, and the demon of anger. Modern readers may interpret these figures psychologically or take them at face value; either way, the wisdom holds. In solitude, we meet the parts of ourselves we've been running from. The desert doesn't create our inner chaos; it reveals it.

And this revelation is precisely the point. You can't heal what you can't see. You can't offer to God what you refuse to acknowledge. The desert, in its terrible mercy, strips away our carefully constructed personas and leaves us naked before the One who loved us before we learned to perform.

The Digital Anti-Desert

If the desert is characterized by emptiness, silence, and confrontation with the self, our digital environment is its precise opposite. It offers endless fullness: an inexhaustible stream of images, words, sounds, opinions, updates, arguments, and entertainments. It fills every gap, colonizes every pause, rushes in to occupy any moment of potential stillness.

The silence that the desert monks cultivated as a garden in which the soul might grow, we've learned to experience as a threat. We call it boredom, and we've developed a thousand ways to avoid it. The average person now checks their phone dozens of times per day, often without conscious intention. We've developed reflexes, not choices. The hand reaches for the device before the mind has decided to reach.

And the confrontation with self that the desert demanded? Our devices offer escape routes in every direction. Feeling anxious? Scroll. Feeling sad? Stream something. Feeling the first stirrings of a complex emotion, a challenging thought, a question about the direction of your life? There's always, always, always something else to click.

This isn't an accident. The attention economy depends on capturing and holding our focus. Billions of dollars and some of the brightest minds of our generation have been deployed to make our devices as compelling, as sticky, as irresistible as possible. We aren't weak-willed failures when we find it hard to put down our phones; we're ordinary humans outmatched by sophisticated systems designed to exploit every vulnerability in our neurology.

The monks who fled to the desert were fleeing a world that made it difficult to attend to God. We face the same challenge, but in an intensified form. The noise has followed us everywhere, even into our beds, even into those first waking moments that once belonged to quietness, even into the final minutes before sleep. There's no geographical desert left to flee to.

And so we must create one.

Sabbath as Resistance

The practice of Sabbath is woven into the very fabric of biblical faith. On the seventh day, God rested, not from exhaustion but from completion, not because the work had worn God out but because the work was good and deserved to be savored. The commandment to keep the Sabbath holy is nestled among the prohibitions against murder and theft, as if the refusal to rest were itself a kind of violence against the soul.

The Sabbath was, for ancient Israel, an act of resistance against the empire of endless production. In Egypt, there had been no rest. Pharaoh demanded bricks without straw, quotas without mercy. The Sabbath declared that the people of God were no longer enslaved people, that their output didn't measure their worth, that they belonged to a different economy altogether, an economy of grace.

We need this resistance now as urgently as Israel needed it then. The digital economy is, in its own way, Pharaoh's Egypt. It demands constant productivity, constant availability, and constant engagement. It has colonized not only our working hours but our leisure, not only our offices but our living rooms and bedrooms. The boundary between work and rest has dissolved; we're always, in some sense, on call.

"The practice of a Tech Sabbath is an act of spiritual defiance. It declares that our connectivity doesn't define us, that our worth doesn't depend on our responsiveness."

The practice of a Tech Sabbath, a regular, rhythmic withdrawal from our devices, is an act of spiritual defiance. It declares that we aren't defined by our connectivity, that our worth doesn't depend on our responsiveness, that there's a Presence more critical than any

26

notification. It's a way of enacting, in the body and in time, the truth that we belong to God.

Designing Your Desert Day

What might a Tech Sabbath actually look like? The specifics will vary according to vocation, family situation, and temperament, but several principles can guide the practice.

First, choose a rhythm. The traditional Sabbath is weekly, and there's wisdom in this frequency. A day each week is long enough to rest genuinely, short enough to be sustainable, and regular enough to reshape our habits over time. For some, a full twenty-four hours may be possible. For others, parents of young children, caregivers, and those in certain professions, a shorter period may be more realistic. Begin where you can, not where you think you should.

Second, prepare practically. If your phone is your alarm clock, buy an alarm clock. If you need to be reachable for genuine emergencies, designate a single person who can contact you by landline or other means. Tell the people who might need you that you'll be unavailable. Handle in advance whatever tasks might otherwise pull you back online. The goal is to remove the practical excuses that will inevitably present themselves.

Third, embrace the emptiness. This is the hardest part. The first hours without a device can feel disorienting, even distressing. You'll reach for your phone, only to find it missing. You'll feel urges to check, to scroll, to fill the silence. This is withdrawal, and it's instructive. Notice how deeply the habit has rooted itself in your body. Notice how uncomfortable stillness has become. This noticing is itself spiritual work.

Fourth, fill the space with life. Sabbath isn't simply about what we refrain from; it's about what we turn toward. Walk outside and attend to the sky. Read a book made of paper. Prepare food slowly, savoring the textures and smells. Sit with people you love and have conversations without the interruption of buzzing pockets. Pray. Sleep. Play. Do the things that make you feel human in ways that scrolling never does.

Fifth, expect resistance. The demons the desert monks encountered will show up in modern dress. Acedia will whisper that this practice is pointless, that you're wasting time, that everyone else is online, and you're missing out. Anxiety will catastrophize about what emergencies might be unfolding without your knowledge. Vainglory will wonder what people will think of your unavailability. These voices are data; they reveal how deeply the digital world has formed your imagination. Thank them for the information, and stay in the desert anyway.

What Happens in the Silence

The desert monks were reluctant to speak of their inner experiences. They knew the dangers of spiritual pride, of making much of one's own progress, of turning the journey toward God into a performance for others. Yet their writings gesture toward a transformation that occurred in those who persevered.

They spoke of *hesychia*, a profound stillness of heart, a quieting of the inner chaos, a peace that was not the absence of struggle but the presence of God in the midst of it. They spoke of *apatheia*, not apathy in our modern sense, but a freedom from the tyranny of disordered passions, a capacity to respond to life from a centered and grounded place. They spoke of *purity of heart*, the simplification of desire until one thing alone was wanted: God.

These gifts don't come quickly. The desert demands time, and time is precisely what our culture is most reluctant to give. But even a single day of withdrawal can begin to loosen the grip of compulsion. Even a few hours of silence can reveal how noisy the soul has become. Even a brief fast from the digital flood can restore some sense of proportion, some capacity for wonder, some awareness of the sacred that the scroll has drowned out.

Many who practice Tech Sabbath report that the world seems different afterward, colors brighter, conversations deeper, food more flavorful, and prayer more possible. This isn't magic; it's the natural result of attention restored. When we stop fragmenting our focus across a thousand tiny stimuli, the focus that remains can penetrate more deeply into whatever is before us. We begin to see again. We begin to hear again. We begin, in some small way, to be present to our own lives.

The Communal Desert

The desert monks were solitary, but they were not alone. They lived in close proximity to one another, gathering for worship, seeking counsel from elders, and sharing the wisdom they had received. The desert was a society of its own kind, a community shaped by shared practices and common purpose.

A Tech Sabbath can be practiced in solitude, but it becomes richer when practiced in community. Families can unplug together and rediscover the lost arts of board games, long walks, and unhurried meals. Churches can encourage the practice, creating a culture of permission in which members support one another's withdrawal from the digital noise. Friends can covenant together, knowing that mutual commitment strengthens individual resolve.

There's something powerful about knowing that others are keeping the same rhythm, that you aren't alone in the desert. The principalities and powers of the attention economy are vast and well-resourced; we need one another to resist them. The witness of a community that regularly unplugs becomes a sign to a frantic world that another way is possible.

The God Who Waits in the Emptiness

Beneath all the practical guidance, beneath the strategies for implementation and the warnings about resistance, there's a more profound truth: the desert isn't empty. It only appears so to eyes trained by the world.

"The desert isn't empty. It only appears so to eyes trained by the world."

The mystics have always known that God isn't found primarily in the noise and activity but in the stillness and receptivity. "Be still," the psalmist commands, "and know that I am God." The prophet Elijah

29

found God not in the wind or the earthquake or the fire but in the sound of sheer silence. The Gospel accounts show Jesus repeatedly withdrawing from crowds, seeking deserted places to pray, modeling for the church the necessity of strategic absence.

The practice of Tech Sabbath is, at its heart, an act of faith: faith that if we create space, Someone will fill it; faith that the silence we fear is actually pregnant with presence; faith that the One who made us knows what we need better than the algorithms that profile our behavior. We step away from the screen and into the arms of a God who has been waiting patiently for us to arrive.

This is the scandal of grace: that we don't have to earn God's attention, that we're already loved, that the frantic activity we use to justify our existence is unnecessary to the One whose love is pure gift. The desert strips away the illusion that we must be productive to be worthy. It returns us to the fundamental truth of our identity as beloved creatures, held in being by a Love that won't let us go.

A Prophetic Practice

In a world of compulsive connectivity, choosing to disconnect is a prophetic act. It embodies a different set of values, a different understanding of what makes life meaningful. It witnesses to a reality that transcends the metrics of engagement and the currencies of attention.

The Desert Fathers and Mothers fled to the wilderness in part because the institutional church had grown too comfortable, too compromised, too captive to the powers of their age. Their withdrawal was a form of social criticism enacted in the body. By leaving, they exposed what they were leaving: a society that had lost its bearings, a church that had forgotten its first love.

Our situation is different in its particulars but similar in its structure. The digital world offers genuine goods, connection, information, creativity, community, but it has also become a system of capture, a means by which our attention is harvested and sold. The tech companies aren't evil, but their business model depends on monopolizing our focus. To withdraw, even periodically, is to declare that we won't be so monopolized.

This isn't Luddism. It's not a rejection of technology as such. The monks who fled to the desert didn't reject all human civilization; they took with them the Scriptures, the practices of prayer, and the wisdom of their elders. A Tech Sabbath is a selective, intentional withdrawal, a way of ensuring that we use our tools and they don't use us.

Beginning the Journey

Perhaps you've read this far and felt a stirring, a recognition of something you've been missing, a longing for the stillness you've lost. Maybe you've also felt resistance, the voice that says you could never do this, that your situation is too demanding, that you're too dependent on your devices to withdraw from them.

Both responses are valid. The longing is the voice of your soul, remembering what it was made for. The resistance is the voice of habit, defending its territory. Neither should be ignored.

Start small if you must. A single morning. A few hours. A walk without your phone. Light a candle. Sit in silence. Notice what arises. You may find demons; you may discover boredom; you may find grief for all the life you've missed while your eyes were fixed on a screen. Stay with it. On the other side of this discomfort lies a spaciousness you've forgotten was possible.

The desert is still there, waiting. It doesn't require a plane ticket or a camel. It requires only the willingness to step away from the noise and into the silence where God has always been speaking.

The ancient seekers found life in the desert. So can you.

The Invitation

We stand at a crossroads. The path of compulsive connectivity stretches before us, well-worn and easy to follow, leading toward exhaustion, fragmentation, and the slow atrophy of our capacity for depth. Another

31

path leads into the desert, harder to walk, less populated, requiring more of us.

"The invitation is simple, though not easy: choose one day. Unplug. Enter the desert. Discover what waits for you there."

This second path is the way of the mystics and the monks, the prophets and the saints. It's the way of Jesus, who knew when to withdraw and when to engage, who modeled for us the rhythm of action and contemplation, presence and absence, word and silence.

The invitation is simple, though not easy: choose one day. Unplug. Enter the desert. Discover what waits for you there.

PART II: AUTOSANCTITY IN PUBLIC LIFE

Part II: Autosanctity in Public Life examines manifestations in the public square: geopolitical power ("Hegemonospheres"), celebrity culture and its failures (Yancey), concrete neighbor-love (housing), and moral complexity that challenges tribal thinking (Venezuela).

3. The Rise of Hegemonospheres: Power Blocs, Patron States, and the New World Disorder

Something fundamental has shifted in how the world organizes itself. The architecture of international relations that emerged from the ashes of the Second World War, refined through the Cold War and triumphantly declared universal after 1991, is fracturing. In its place, we're witnessing the emergence of what we might call hegemonospheres: distinct zones of influence where major powers shape the political, economic, and informational realities of their client states. The United States, China, and Russia each anchor their own gravitational field, pulling neighboring nations into orbits of dependency, allegiance, and shared fate.

This piece explores what hegemonospheres are, how they function, and what their rise means for the world we're entering. It also considers how people of faith, and Christians in particular, might orient themselves within this emerging reality.

Defining Hegemonospheres

Before proceeding further, it's worth pausing to define the central term of this piece. A hegemonosphere is a zone of political, economic, and informational influence dominated by a single major power. The word fuses "hegemony," the Greek term for leadership or dominance that Antonio Gramsci adapted to describe how ruling groups maintain power through consent as well as coercion, with "sphere," evoking the spatial and bounded nature of these zones.

The term deliberately echoes the older concept of "spheres of influence" while signaling something distinct. Traditional spheres of influence implied relatively passive zones where great powers agreed not to interfere with each other's interests (or used "soft power" to do so). Hegemonospheres are more active and totalizing. They involve the construction of integrated systems: economic dependencies, security architectures, information environments, and shared narratives that bind client states to their patrons in dense webs of obligation and alignment.

I considered other terms while writing this piece. "Patron geometries" captures something important that "hegemonospheres" doesn't: the variety of shapes these arrangements take. The American network of alliances looks different from China's hub-and-spoke model of bilateral relationships, which differs again from Russia's coercive integration of its near abroad. "Geometries" suggests this variation, while "patron" emphasizes the personal, almost feudal quality of the relationships involved, the exchange of protection for loyalty that echoes medieval lordship and Renaissance patronage.

Yet "hegemonospheres" won out for its immediacy and its emphasis on bounded space. We're witnessing the emergence of distinct worlds, each with its own center of gravity, its own rules of membership, its own internal logic. The spatial metaphor matters. These are territories, even if their borders are fuzzy and contested. To live within a hegemonosphere is to inhabit a particular political universe, shaped by forces emanating from a distant capital.

The term is new, but the reality it describes has historical precedents: the tributary systems of imperial China, the colonial empires of European powers, the Cold War blocs organized around Washington and Moscow. What distinguishes contemporary hegemonospheres is their combination of economic integration, information control, and security dependence into comprehensive systems of alignment.

Understanding this combination is essential to grasping the world now taking shape.

The Crumbling of the Rules-Based Order

The post-1945 international system was built on a remarkable premise: that sovereign states, however unequal in power, would relate to one another through shared institutions and codified rules. The United Nations, the Bretton Woods institutions, the World Trade Organization, and a dense web of treaties and conventions were designed to constrain the strong and protect the weak. Wars of conquest would be illegitimate. Borders would be sacrosanct. Disputes would be adjudicated, not fought.

This system was always imperfect. The great powers retained veto authority in the Security Council. The United States intervened where it wished, from Vietnam to Iraq, often without legal sanction. The Soviet Union crushed dissent within its sphere. Yet the normative framework persisted. Even those who violated the rules felt compelled to justify their violations in the language of the rules themselves.

That pretense is now collapsing. Russia's annexation of Crimea in 2014 and its full-scale invasion of Ukraine in 2022 represented an explicit rejection of the post-war territorial settlement. China's construction of military installations in disputed waters and its assertion of historical claims over Taiwan signal a similar willingness to redraw maps by force. The United States, for its part, has grown selective about which international institutions it supports and which it undermines, withdrawing from agreements and imposing unilateral sanctions that bypass multilateral frameworks. Its military strike on Venezuela highlights its growing hegemonic orientation in its region.

What replaces the rules-based order is something older and more brutal: a world where power determines outcomes, where might makes right, and where smaller states must seek protection from larger ones or face the consequences of isolation.

The institutions remain standing, but their authority drains away. The United Nations Security Council meets, passes resolutions, and watches them ignored. The World Trade Organization issues rulings that major powers decline to implement. International courts hand down judgments that go unenforced. The architecture of global governance has become a stage set, impressive from a distance but hollow upon closer inspection.

Blocs Built on Power, Not Ideology

The Cold War divided the world along ideological lines. Capitalism and communism offered competing visions of human flourishing, and nations aligned themselves accordingly. The struggle was about ideas, systems, and ways of organizing society.

The hegemonospheres emerging today operate on different logic. China doesn't demand that its partners adopt Marxism-Leninism or any particular political system. Russia cultivates relationships with monarchies, democracies, and military juntas alike. Even the United States, which still speaks the language of democracy promotion, has grown comfortable with authoritarian allies when strategic interests align.

What binds these blocs together is interest and dependency, not conviction. A nation joins a hegemonosphere because it needs security guarantees, market access, infrastructure investment, or protection from rivals. The patron provides; the client complies. Ideology becomes a thin veneer over transactions of power.

This represents a profound shift. The twentieth century's great conflicts, for all their horror, were animated by genuine disagreements about how human beings should live. The hegemonospheres of the twenty-first century ask a simpler question: who offers the best deal?

The Economics of Loyalty

Each hegemonosphere has developed its own currency of allegiance. Understanding these transactional mechanics reveals much about how the new order functions.

China's primary instrument is infrastructure debt. Through the Belt and Road Initiative and its various successors, Beijing offers developing nations something they desperately want: roads, ports, railways, and power plants. The loans come with conditions, and the projects are often built by Chinese firms using Chinese labor. When countries can't repay, they find themselves in long-term arrangements that give China strategic assets and political leverage. Sri Lanka's Hambantota Port, leased to China for ninety-nine years after a debt default, has become the emblematic case.

The United States wields different tools. Dollar dominance means that access to the global financial system runs through American banks and clearinghouses. Sanctions can cripple economies overnight. Security guarantees and weapons sales bind allies in webs of military dependency. The implicit bargain: align with Washington and gain access to markets, technology, and protection; defy it and face exclusion.

Russia operates with cruder instruments. Energy dependency has long been Moscow's lever over Europe and Central Asia. Military intervention, whether through official forces or mercenary groups like the former Wagner, offers embattled governments survival in exchange for resource concessions and political loyalty. Where China builds and America sanctions, Russia threatens and protects.

The result is that loyalty is purchased differently across hegemonospheres. A nation bound to China through debt feels different pressures than one dependent on American security guarantees or Russian energy supplies. The texture of clienthood varies, even as the underlying structure of patron-client relations remains consistent.

These economic relationships create path dependencies. Once a nation's infrastructure is built with Chinese loans, its maintenance requires Chinese expertise. Once an economy is structured around access to American markets, reorientation becomes costly. Once energy grids depend on Russian gas, alternatives take years to develop. The initial transaction locks in future alignment, making exit from a hegemonosphere progressively more difficult.

Strongmen and the Death of Neutrality

Within each hegemonosphere, power increasingly concentrates in the hands of individual leaders. Xi Jinping has abolished term limits and accumulated authority unseen since Mao. Vladimir Putin's Russia is a personalist autocracy where institutions exist to serve the leader. Even in the democratic West, the appeal of strongman politics has grown, with leaders who promise to cut through institutional constraints and act decisively.

This personalization of power matters because it shapes how hegemonospheres operate. Decisions flow from the top. Relationships between blocs become relationships between leaders. The system grows more volatile, more dependent on the temperament and judgment of a few individuals, more susceptible to miscalculation.

For smaller states, the rise of hegemonospheres has made neutrality increasingly untenable. Switzerland and Sweden, long bastions of non-alignment, have reconsidered their positions in the wake of Russia's invasion of Ukraine. Finland abandoned decades of careful neutrality to join NATO. The pressure to choose sides intensifies as the spaces between blocs shrink.

Some middle powers have found room to maneuver. Turkey plays NATO membership against relationships with Russia and overtures to China. India maintains strategic partnerships with both Washington and Moscow. Saudi Arabia and the Gulf states leverage their energy resources to maintain autonomy. Brazil and Indonesia position themselves as voices of a Global South that refuses to align fully with any hegemonosphere. Yet this maneuvering space may be temporary. As great power competition intensifies, the pressure to choose will grow.

Complicating this picture is the role of private power. Mercenary groups, technology platforms, sovereign wealth funds, and multinational corporations operate within and across hegemonospheres according to their own logic. The Wagner Group extended Russian influence in Africa through contracts that bypassed state-to-state relations. American tech companies shape information environments worldwide while pursuing profit, not policy. These actors are neither fully independent nor fully controlled, creating a layer of complexity that traditional analyses of state power often miss.

Echoes of Empire

There is something familiar about all this. The language of hegemonospheres deliberately echoes older patterns: tributary systems, suzerainty, spheres of influence, patron-client relations. We've been here before.

Imperial China presided over a tributary system in East Asia for centuries. Neighboring kingdoms acknowledged the emperor's supremacy, sent tribute missions, and received in return recognition, trade privileges, and protection. The relationship was hierarchical and ritualized, but it provided stability.

European colonialism created a different pattern: direct extraction backed by military force. Gunboat diplomacy compelled weaker nations to open their markets and accept unequal treaties. The colonial powers did not seek tribute; they sought resources, labor, and captive markets.

Today's hegemonospheres blend elements of both models. China's debt diplomacy has been compared to neo-colonialism, with infrastructure projects serving as vehicles for resource extraction and political control. American military bases encircle the globe in patterns that recall imperial garrisons. Russia's interventions in its near abroad echo tsarist and Soviet domination of borderlands.

The resonances with colonialism raise uncomfortable questions. Has the post-colonial era ended? Were the decades of formal sovereign equality an interlude, now closing? The new arrangements may lack the explicit racism of nineteenth-century imperialism, but they reproduce its structural inequalities. Client states have flags and seats at the United Nations, yet their sovereignty is constrained by the requirements of their patrons.

Which historical analogy illuminates our moment most clearly? The nineteenth-century Concert of Europe, where great powers managed their competition through periodic conferences and recognized spheres of influence? The Cold War, now with three players instead of two? The tributary systems of imperial China, with their hierarchies of recognition and ritual? Each comparison captures something, and each breaks down at crucial points. Perhaps hegemonospheres represent a genuinely novel configuration, drawing on historical patterns while creating something new.

Information Sovereignty and Parallel Realities

One feature distinguishes contemporary hegemonospheres from their historical predecessors: the construction of separate information environments. Each bloc increasingly inhabits its own reality, with its own facts, narratives, and interpretive frameworks.

China's Great Firewall creates a digital space largely sealed from the global internet. Chinese citizens access different platforms, encounter different news, and operate within different parameters of acceptable discourse. Russia has moved in the same direction, blocking foreign media and cultivating domestic alternatives while projecting its narrative outward through state-funded channels.

The Western hegemonosphere maintains its own information architecture, dominated by American technology platforms that shape what billions of people see and discuss. These platforms are neither neutral nor universal; they encode particular assumptions about speech, privacy, and community that reflect their origins.

The fragmentation of the information environment means that people living in different hegemonospheres may lack common reference points. Events are interpreted through incompatible frames. Shared facts become scarce. The possibility of meaningful dialogue across bloc lines diminishes.

This information fragmentation enables something that would have seemed impossible a generation ago: the provision of legitimacy

41

without democracy. The liberal assumption that authoritarian systems were inherently unstable, that populations would inevitably demand political freedom as they grew richer, appears increasingly doubtful. China offers a model of authoritarian capitalism that delivers growth, stability, and national pride. Russia wraps its autocracy in the language of traditional values and resistance to Western decadence. For many populations, these offerings prove attractive. The hegemonospheres can provide order, development, and meaning without elections.

The Grey Zones

Where hegemonospheres meet, friction zones emerge. Ukraine has become the bloodiest example: a nation caught between Russian claims to its territory and Western support for its sovereignty. The war there is, in one sense, a contest over which hegemonosphere Ukraine will belong to.

Taiwan occupies a similar position in East Asia. The island exists in a state of ambiguity, claimed by China, protected by the United States, and governed by its own democratic institutions. Any resolution will determine the boundaries of the Chinese and American hegemonospheres in the Pacific.

The South China Sea, the Sahel, the Caucasus, Central Asia: these regions have become arenas of great power competition, places where hegemonospheres contest for influence. The human cost falls on those who live there, caught between forces they can't control.

Buffer states and grey zones have always existed between empires. What is new is the intensity of the competition and the global stakes involved. The integration of the world economy means that conflicts in these friction zones ripple outward, disrupting supply chains, displacing populations, and destabilizing regions far from the fighting.

What the Client States Want

Analysis of hegemonospheres tends to focus on the great powers, their strategies and ambitions. But the client states aren't passive objects. They've their own interests, their own calculations, their own agency within constraints.

Security ranks high among client state priorities. A government facing internal insurgency or external threats may accept constraints on its sovereignty in exchange for military support. This is the bargain that many African states have struck with Russia, and that others maintain with the United States or France.

Development is another draw. Countries that need infrastructure, investment, and access to markets may find that aligning with a major power opens doors. China's appeal in much of the Global South stems from its willingness to build things, to provide capital, and to do so without the governance conditions that Western institutions often attach.

Some client states seek cultural preservation or ideological validation. Alignment with a hegemonosphere can protect traditional values against what some see as Western cultural imperialism, or conversely, can affiliate a nation with liberal democratic norms it wishes to embrace.

The view from the client state isn't one of helpless subordination. It's one of constrained choice, of selecting among imperfect options, of navigating a world where independence is limited but not extinguished.

Implications for the World Ahead

The rise of hegemonospheres points toward a world that looks less like the liberal international order imagined after 1991 and more like the multipolar competitions of earlier centuries. Several implications follow.

First, global governance will weaken. Institutions that require consensus among great powers will struggle to function when those powers see each other as adversaries. Climate agreements, pandemic response, nuclear non-proliferation: all become harder when the major players are locked in strategic competition.

Second, economic decoupling will accelerate. Supply chains will reorganize along bloc lines. Technology ecosystems will fragment. The efficiency gains of globalization will be sacrificed to the security imperatives of hegemonospheric competition.

Third, military spending will rise. The great powers are already rearming, and their client states will follow. Resources that might have gone to development, health, or education will flow instead to weapons and defenses.

Fourth, the risk of major war increases. The grey zones where hegemonospheres meet are inherently unstable. Miscalculation, escalation, and the logic of credibility could draw great powers into direct conflict. The nuclear dimension makes such conflict potentially catastrophic.

This isn't an optimistic forecast. But it may be a realistic one.

How Should People of Faith Respond?

The emergence of hegemonospheres poses profound questions for religious communities, and for Christians in particular. How should people of faith orient themselves in a world of competing power blocs?

One theological question underlies all others: what is the proper scale of human political organization? Scripture offers no blueprint for international relations. The Bible contains stories of empires and small kingdoms, of conquest and exile, of prophets who condemned the powerful and comforted the oppressed. Christians have lived under every form of government and within every kind of political arrangement.

Some will argue that the nation-state deserves Christian loyalty, that the particular communities into which we're born carry divine significance. Others will insist that the Church transcends all political boundaries, that Christians owe ultimate allegiance to a kingdom not of this world. Still others will seek a middle path, acknowledging legitimate

44

claims of nations while maintaining a prophetic distance from all earthly powers.

What seems clear is that Christians can't simply baptize any hegemonosphere as godly. The temptation to identify faith with national or civilizational projects has led to grievous errors throughout history. The church that becomes a chaplain to empire loses its prophetic voice.

At the same time, Christians can't withdraw entirely from political engagement. The call to seek the welfare of the city where God has placed us, to pursue justice, to care for the vulnerable, requires participation in the structures of power, however flawed.

This participation must include resistance to the injustices that hegemonospheres inevitably produce. Every system of concentrated power generates victims: the populations displaced by proxy wars in grey zones, the workers exploited in supply chains organized for the patron's benefit, the dissidents silenced to maintain a client government's stability, the communities impoverished by debt arrangements they never chose. People of faith have a particular obligation to see these victims, to name the structures that harm them, and to stand with them even when doing so is costly. The prophetic tradition runs deep in Judaism, Christianity, and Islam alike: a insistence that God sides with the oppressed, that no political arrangement is beyond moral judgment, that the powerful will be called to account. Hegemonospheres may be facts of geopolitical life, but they aren't morally neutral facts. They require scrutiny, critique, and where possible, reform. The person of faith asks not only "how do I navigate this system?" but "what does justice demand of me within it?"

Perhaps the most important witness Christians can offer in an age of hegemonospheres is the practice of transnational solidarity. The global Church spans every bloc. Christians in America, China, Russia, and the client states of each hegemonosphere share a common faith and a common Lord. Maintaining those bonds of fellowship across political lines, refusing to let geopolitical competition sever spiritual communion, would be a powerful testimony.

Other religious traditions will find their own resources for navigating this terrain. Islam's ummah transcends national boundaries. Buddhism's teaching on impermanence relativizes all political arrangements. Judaism's experience of diaspora offers wisdom about maintaining identity within hostile or indifferent empires. Each tradition brings something to the conversation about how to live faithfully in a world of competing powers.

Living in the Interregnum

We're living in an interregnum: the old order is dying, and the new order isn't yet fully born. The rules-based international system has not vanished, but it no longer commands universal assent. Hegemonospheres are forming, but their boundaries remain contested and their internal structures unstable.

The term hegemonosphere is itself an attempt to name what is happening, to provide a conceptual handle for a reality that resists easy description. Whether this particular word gains currency matters less than the underlying recognition: that the world is reorganizing into distinct zones of power, that the old certainties are fading, and that we must learn to navigate a more dangerous and divided landscape.

Understanding hegemonospheres is a first step. The harder work lies ahead: building institutions that can function across bloc lines, maintaining human connections that transcend political divisions, and holding fast to values that no hegemon can claim as its exclusive property. In this work, people of all faiths and none have a stake. The alternative is a world fragmented into hostile camps, armed to the teeth, and lurching toward catastrophe.

We've been here before. Humanity has survived eras of imperial competition, great power rivalry, and civilizational conflict. But we've also witnessed the devastation that such eras can bring. The rise of hegemonospheres is an invitation to learn from history, to build bridges where walls are rising, and to remember that the divisions we create are never as permanent as they seem.

4. Philip Yancey, Celebrity, Brokenness, and Me

Philip Yancey shaped my faith. His books on grace, pain, and the mysteries of God met me in seasons when I needed language for experiences I couldn't articulate. When I learned about his eight-year affair and its recent exposure, something in me collapsed. I suspect I'm not alone.

I've been sitting with this news, asking what it means for those of us who trusted his words, for the church that elevated him, and for the wider crisis of leadership that his fall represents. I've also been asking what it means for me, because I know the soil from which this kind of failure grows. I've tasted my own versions of self-deception and the gap between public persona and private reality.

This piece is an attempt to think through what happened, what it reveals, and where we go from here.

What Happened

The reported facts are devastating in their plainness. For eight years, Yancey maintained a secret relationship while continuing to write and speak about grace, faithfulness, and the Christian life. Eight years is a sustained pattern of choices, a daily architecture of deception that had to be actively maintained. This wasn't a moment of weakness or a single catastrophic lapse. It was a parallel life.

What does that kind of ongoing duplicity do to a person's soul? To their other relationships? To the creative and spiritual work produced during that period? These are questions without easy answers, but they deserve honest attention.

And then there's Janet, his wife of decades. The spouses of fallen leaders often become invisible in these conversations, their pain subsumed into the larger narrative about the famous person. She deserves acknowledgment, even from strangers who will never know the contours of her experience.

The Parasocial Bond

Those of us who read Yancey's books developed a peculiar kind of relationship with him. Through his vulnerable, searching prose, we felt we knew him. His doubts became companions to our doubts. His tentative articulations of grace became scaffolding for our own fragile faith.

This is the parasocial dynamic: an intimate emotional connection with someone we've never met, mediated entirely through their public work. It's real in its effects, even if it's illusory in its foundation. We mourn something genuine when we learn the person we thought we knew was, in significant ways, performing.

What do we do with the books now? The passages we underlined, the chapters we pressed into the hands of struggling friends? I don't think we need to burn them. The words that helped us still helped us. The truths about grace remain true even when spoken by someone who failed to embody them. But the relationship changes. We read differently now, with a kind of protective distance.

The Grace Writer's Fall

There's a painful irony here that deserves direct attention. Philip Yancey made grace accessible to millions of readers. He wrote about it with a theological depth and emotional honesty that few have matched. And now he needs it in the most public, most humiliating way imaginable.

Does his writing still mean something? I think so. Grace was always, by definition, for failures and hypocrites. It was never a reward

48

for the consistent. Yancey himself made this point repeatedly. The doctrine hasn't changed because the messenger proved to need it as desperately as anyone.

And yet something feels different when the writer of grace books is revealed to have been living a lie while writing them. The words came from a divided heart, a compartmentalized life. They were true, but they were also, in some sense, a performance. That complexity is hard to hold.

The Trust Problem

For those of us who care about the church's witness and credibility, Yancey's fall creates yet another entry in a long and devastating ledger. Christian leaders have been failing publicly for decades: financial scandals, sexual abuse, affairs, bullying, spiritual manipulation. Each revelation erodes trust a little further.

What makes the trust problem particularly acute is the church's posture on sexual ethics. Christianity has, in recent decades, made sexuality one of its primary battlegrounds in the culture wars. We have criticized, condemned, and campaigned. We have positioned ourselves as the guardians of sexual morality in a decadent society.

And then the royal commissions revealed systematic child abuse. And the megachurch pastors fell one after another. And the youth leaders were exposed. And the beloved author who wrote about grace was living a double life for nearly a decade.

The gap between our collective moral pronouncements and our collective moral failures has become a chasm. We've lost the right to speak from a position of moral authority on these matters. This doesn't mean sexual ethics don't matter. They matter profoundly. But we need a different posture: humility rather than judgment, solidarity with sinning people rather than condemnation of them, honesty about our own failures before we point to others.

Celebrity and the Platform Problem

The modern church has built an infrastructure of celebrity. We have stages and green rooms and bestseller lists. We have podcast downloads and conference circuits and social media followings. We have created a class of Christian famous people and given them extraordinary influence over millions of lives.

This platform system is, in many ways, a setup for failure. It isolates leaders from normal accountability. It creates enormous pressure to maintain a public image. It generates the kind of power imbalance that makes exploitation possible and exposure unlikely. It selects for charisma and productivity over character and stability.

Yancey, by all accounts, was one of the good ones: humble, thoughtful, not given to the obvious excesses of the celebrity pastor archetype. And still the system failed him, or he failed within it. What does that tell us about the system itself?

Who knew about his affair? Who should have known? What accountability structures were in place, and why did they fail? These questions matter because the answers might help us build something better. Authors who work alone, traveling constantly, answering to no one, are uniquely vulnerable. We need to ask what meaningful accountability even looks like for people in that position.

The Exhausting Cycle

Why does this keep happening? Every few months, another leader, another scandal, another round of shock and grief and think pieces. Is there something structurally wrong with how we form and deploy Christian leaders? Or is this simply human nature meeting power and opportunity?

I suspect it's both. Human beings are remarkably capable of self-deception, compartmentalization, and rationalization. Put us in positions of unchecked influence, remove normal social accountability, give us adoring audiences and demanding schedules, and failure becomes statistically likely. The surprise is anyone surviving the system with integrity intact.

This doesn't excuse individual responsibility. Yancey made choices. He chose deception every day for eight years. But the system he operated within made those choices easier to make and harder to catch. Both things are true.

Standing in the Same Soil

I can't write about Yancey's failure from a position of comfortable distance. I know the soil from which this kind of collapse grows. I've seen it in my own life.

I've been an alcoholic. I've been a workaholic who sacrificed my family on the altar of ministry productivity. I've craved recognition and platform in ways that distorted my priorities. My marriage ended in divorce. I have wounded people I was supposed to care for.

The specific manifestations differ, but the underlying dynamics feel familiar: the capacity for self-deception, the gap between public image and private reality, the way ambition can masquerade as calling, the slow drift into compromise that happens so gradually you barely notice until you're somewhere you never intended to be.

I don't say this to excuse anyone, least of all myself. I say it because honesty requires it. I am writing about leadership failure as someone who has failed in leadership. I am writing about brokenness as someone who is broken. Whatever critique I offer of Yancey or the church is offered from inside the problem, as a participant in the very dynamics I'm describing.

What Our Brokenness Teaches Us

If there's a thread connecting all of this, it's the revelation of human brokenness. We are all, every one of us, less integrated than we appear. We all have gaps between who we present and who we are in private. We are all capable of sustained self-deception in the service of desires we're ashamed to acknowledge.

The Christian tradition has a word for this: sin. It's an unfashionable word, but it names something real about our condition. We are bent. We are divided against ourselves. We need help from outside ourselves to become whole.

This is where grace re-enters the conversation. Grace is the claim that God meets us in our brokenness, that we don't have to pretend to be whole to be loved. Grace is what makes honesty possible, because the stakes of exposure are lowered. You already know the worst about me, and you haven't left.

Yancey wrote about this. He wrote about it beautifully. And now he needs it to be true for him in the most concrete, most uncomfortable way. So do I. So do you.

Lessons for the Church

What should we learn from this? I want to offer some tentative suggestions, knowing that I offer them as someone who has contributed to the problems I'm describing.

First, we need to dismantle the celebrity system. Christian leadership should be local, accountable, plural, and temporary. The stages and platforms create more problems than they solve. We should be deeply suspicious of any structure that concentrates spiritual authority in charismatic individuals with national or international reach.

Second, we need to change our posture on sexual ethics. We can hold strong convictions about sexuality while speaking from humility and solidarity with those struggling with sin and brokenness. We should be the last to condemn, not the first. We have forfeited the right to moral pronouncement through our collective failures.

Third, we need real accountability structures with teeth. This means relationships where leaders are known, truly known, by people who have both the access and the authority to intervene. It means systems that don't rely on famous people self-reporting their struggles.

Fourth, we need to stop being surprised. Human beings fail. Leaders fail. Christians fail. This should be built into our ecclesiology from the ground up. We should design our communities to catch falls, not to pretend they won't happen.

Fifth, we need to care for the wounded. Janet Yancey. The woman involved in the affair. The readers whose faith was shaped by his books. The staff and friends and colleagues who feel betrayed. These people need pastoral care, not just public commentary.

A Word to Fellow Leaders

If you're in Christian leadership, this should terrify you. I don't mean that in a paralyzing way. I mean it should wake you up. If Philip Yancey could maintain an eight-year deception while writing some of the most beloved Christian books of our generation, what makes you think you're immune?

Are you known? Really known? Does anyone have access to the parts of your life you'd prefer to keep hidden? Do you have relationships where you can be honest about your temptations before they become actions?

I have failed in leadership. I know how easy it is to let the gap between public and private widen. I know the rationalizations, the slow compromises, the way busyness can become a cover for avoidance. If you're drifting, now is the time to turn around. Today. Before another year passes. Before the parallel life becomes so established that you can't imagine dismantling it.

Grace Persists

I don't know how to end this piece neatly. There's no resolution that makes the pain go away or restores what was lost. Philip Yancey failed. The church has failed repeatedly. I have failed. We are all implicated in a system that produces these outcomes with depressing regularity.

And yet grace persists. The claim at the center of our faith is that failure isn't final, that brokenness can be met with healing, that even the most sustained deceptions can be brought into the light and forgiven.

This is either true or it isn't. If it's true, it's true for Yancey. It's true for me. It's true for all of us.

The question is whether we'll build communities that embody this grace, not as a cheap excuse for ongoing failure, but as the foundation for genuine transformation. Communities where honesty is possible because judgment is suspended. Where accountability exists because love is real. Where leaders are human beings, fully known and fully loved, rather than platforms projecting images into the void.

I don't know if we'll get there. But I know we have to try.

5. A Place to Call Home: Why Affordable Housing Demands Church and Society's Urgent Attention

In cities across Australia and the United States, and in much of the world, families are making impossible choices. A single mother in Sydney decides between paying rent and buying groceries. A retired couple in Phoenix watches their fixed income shrink as housing costs rise. A young teacher in Melbourne commutes two hours each way because affordable housing near her school has vanished. These stories repeat themselves millions of times over, forming a quiet crisis that reshapes communities, fractures families, and leaves lasting wounds on human dignity.

Housing has become one of the defining moral challenges of our time. The church has historically responded to such challenges with prophetic voice and practical action, building hospitals and schools, feeding the hungry, and welcoming the stranger. Today, housing insecurity calls for the same response. This is a matter of urgent priority for religious communities, a primary social and spiritual issue that touches the foundations of human flourishing, and an area where religious organizations can work alongside government and civil society to achieve meaningful change.

The Sacred Significance of Shelter

Scripture repeatedly speaks about dwelling places, the significance of home, and the tragedy of displacement. The Hebrew scriptures contain detailed instructions about housing the stranger and protecting those who lack secure shelter. Deuteronomy's vision of a just society includes provisions to ensure that no family permanently loses its ancestral land. The prophets thundered against those who accumulated houses while others had none, with Isaiah condemning those who "join house to house" until no space remains for people with low incomes.[9]

Jesus himself experienced housing precarity. Born in borrowed space because there was no room at the inn, raised as a refugee fleeing to Egypt, and later declaring that "the Son of Man has nowhere to lay his head," Christ knew the vulnerability of displacement. His ministry consistently elevated hospitality as a central virtue, from staying in the homes of both tax collectors and religious leaders to his parable of the Good Samaritan, which pivots on providing shelter to a stranger in need.

Catholic social teaching has developed extensive frameworks connecting housing to human dignity. Pope Leo XIII's Rerum Novarum in 1891 defended the right to property while insisting on its social obligations. Subsequent encyclicals have consistently affirmed that housing security is essential to family life, child development, and community participation. The Compendium of the Social Doctrine of the Church states that access to adequate housing is among the conditions necessary for human dignity.[10] Protestant traditions have similarly emphasized stewardship, economic justice, and care for the vulnerable as theological imperatives bearing directly on housing questions.

At its core, the theological case for housing rests on a simple conviction: every person bears the image of God and deserves conditions that allow human flourishing. Stable housing enables families to form lasting bonds, children to develop in consistent environments, communities to build the trust that makes civic life possible, and

---

[9] Isaiah 5:8 (ESV): "Woe to those who join house to house, who add field to field, until there is no more room, and you are made to dwell alone in the midst of the land."
[10] Pontifical Council for Justice and Peace, *Compendium of the Social Doctrine of the Church*, §482.

individuals to participate fully in a religious community. When housing becomes precarious, all of these goods are threatened.

Housing Insecurity as Spiritual Crisis

The practical harms of housing instability are well documented: poor health outcomes, disrupted education, reduced employment prospects, and increased rates of family breakdown. But the spiritual dimensions deserve equal attention. Housing precarity erodes the conditions necessary for spiritual formation. Constant worry about next month's rent or the possibility of eviction creates chronic stress that crowds out the contemplative space prayer requires. Frequent moves fracture the relationships that sustain faith communities. When families must choose between housing and other necessities, church involvement often becomes a casualty.

"When housing becomes precarious, the conditions necessary for spiritual formation erode. Constant worry about next month's rent crowds out the contemplative space prayer requires. Frequent moves fracture the relationships that sustain faith communities. When families must choose between housing and other necessities, church involvement often becomes a casualty."

Congregations feel these effects directly. Churches in gentrifying neighborhoods watch longtime members displaced to distant suburbs, breaking bonds built over decades. Pastors report spending increasing time helping parishioners navigate housing crises. Young families who might form the next generation of church leadership struggle to establish themselves in communities where housing costs consume unsustainable portions of their income.

The psychological toll compounds these challenges. Research consistently links housing insecurity to depression, anxiety, and diminished hope. Children who experience housing instability show elevated rates of behavioral problems and reduced academic achievement. For adults, the shame associated with housing struggles often leads to social withdrawal, including withdrawal from religious communities that might otherwise provide support. The crisis feeds on itself: those who most need community support become increasingly isolated from it.

Understanding the Crisis: Australia and the United States

The Australian Context

Australia faces a housing crisis of historic proportions. Median house prices in Sydney and Melbourne now exceed ten times median household income, placing homeownership beyond reach for most young families without parental assistance. Rental vacancy rates hover near record lows in most capital cities, giving landlords enormous power and leaving renters with few options when facing rent increases or eviction.

The consequences appear in stark statistics. Over 120,000 Australians experience homelessness on any given night, with the number growing steadily.[11] More than a million households experience rental stress, defined as paying more than 30% of income on housing costs. Waitlists for public housing stretch into years and sometimes decades, with some states reporting wait times exceeding fifteen years for applicants without urgent priority status.[12]

Structural factors drive this crisis. Negative gearing provisions allow property investors to offset rental losses against other income, creating tax advantages that encourage investment in existing housing stock. Capital gains tax concessions favor property investment over different assets. Population growth, concentrated heavily in Sydney and Melbourne, has outpaced new housing construction. Planning restrictions limit density in established suburbs, pushing development to the urban fringes, where infrastructure and services are inadequate. Public housing stock has declined as a proportion of total housing for decades, leaving a shrinking safety net.

---

[11] Australian Bureau of Statistics, "Estimating Homelessness: Census 2021."
[12] Mission Australia, "Response to Report on Government Services 2024: Housing and Homelessness."

The United States faces parallel challenges with distinctive features. Homelessness has reached levels unseen in decades, with over 770,000 people experiencing homelessness on a single night.[13] In cities like Los Angeles, San Francisco, and New York, encampments have become permanent features of the urban landscape. Rural homelessness, less visible but equally devastating, affects thousands more.

The affordable housing shortage extends far beyond those experiencing homelessness. The National Low Income Housing Coalition estimates a shortage of over seven million affordable rental units for extremely low-income households.[14] For every one hundred such households, only thirty-three affordable units exist.[15] This gap forces families into housing that consumes unsustainable portions of their income, into overcrowded conditions, or onto the streets.

American housing policy has retreated from its mid-century commitments. Federal investment in public housing has declined dramatically since the 1980s, leaving many public housing authorities managing aging, deteriorating stock. The Housing Choice Voucher program, which subsidizes private-market rentals for low-income families, serves only about one-quarter of eligible households due to funding limitations.[16] Exclusionary zoning in wealthy communities restricts multifamily housing construction, maintaining patterns of economic and racial segregation while constraining supply.

Why the Church Has a Distinctive Role

Religious organizations bring unique assets to housing challenges. Churches hold significant land, often in established neighborhoods with good access to transport and services. Many congregations occupy sites

---

[13] U.S. Department of Housing and Urban Development, *The 2024 Annual Homeless Assessment Report (AHAR) to Congress, Part 1*.
[14] National Low Income Housing Coalition, *The Gap: A Shortage of Affordable Homes*.
[15] National Low Income Housing Coalition, *The Gap: A Shortage of Affordable Homes*.
[16] Center on Budget and Policy Priorities, "Federal Rental Assistance Fact Sheets."

far larger than their current ministry requires, with parking lots empty six days a week and buildings underutilized. This real estate represents an extraordinary resource for affordable housing development.

"Churches hold significant land, often in established neighborhoods with good access to transport and services. Many congregations occupy sites far larger than their current ministry requires, with parking lots empty six days a week and buildings underutilized. This real estate represents an extraordinary resource for affordable housing development."

Beyond physical assets, churches possess moral authority. Congregations can speak from a platform of values rather than interests, advocating for policies that may not benefit their members directly but serve the common good. Religious leaders have historically played crucial roles in movements for social change, from abolition to civil rights. The housing crisis calls for similar moral leadership.

Churches also maintain a long-term presence in communities. While businesses come and go and government priorities shift with electoral cycles, many congregations have served the same neighborhoods for generations. This stability enables patient, sustained engagement with complex social problems. Churches can make commitments that span decades, the timeframe housing solutions often require.

Finally, congregations constitute networks of relationships and care. When families face housing crises, church communities often provide immediate support: meals, temporary accommodation, financial assistance, and emotional sustenance. These informal networks catch many who would otherwise fall through official safety nets. Yet charity alone can't solve structural problems, and religious communities must couple direct service with advocacy for systemic change.

Practical Pathways: Australia

Policy Reforms Worth Supporting

Several policy reforms could significantly improve housing affordability in Australia, and churches can advocate for these changes. Increased investment in public and community housing tops the list. Australia's social housing stock has declined as a proportion of total housing for decades, and rebuilding this stock requires sustained government commitment. State and federal governments should establish long-term funding streams for social housing construction, potentially through dedicated levies or bonds.

Tax reform remains contentious but necessary. Negative gearing and capital gains tax concessions direct investment toward existing housing rather than new construction, inflating prices while doing little to increase supply. Phasing out these provisions, with grandfathering for existing investments, would redirect capital toward more productive uses. Build-to-rent developments, where institutional investors construct and manage rental housing, could be encouraged through favorable tax treatment that includes affordability requirements.

Planning reform offers another avenue. Many local councils resist density in established suburbs, pushing development to the urban fringes, where infrastructure costs are high, and services are sparse. State governments can override local resistance to ensure adequate housing construction near transport and employment centers. Inclusionary zoning, which requires developers to include affordable units in new projects, has shown promise in other jurisdictions.

What Australian Churches Can Do

Australian churches hold substantial property assets that could be mobilized for affordable housing. Denominational property trusts should audit their holdings and identify sites suitable for development. Partnerships with community housing providers allow churches to contribute land while professional organizations handle development and management. Several Australian dioceses and denominations have already embarked on such partnerships, creating models that others can follow.

Congregational advocacy matters enormously. Politicians respond to constituent pressure, and churches can organize members to engage with housing policy at the local, state, and federal levels. Writing letters, attending community meetings, meeting with elected representatives, and supporting candidates who prioritize housing affordability all contribute to political change. Denominational social justice bodies can coordinate these efforts across congregations.

Direct service continues to matter. Churches can support organizations working on homelessness, contribute to rental assistance programs, and offer space for services that connect people with housing resources. Some congregations have established housing ministries that help families navigate the complex landscape of assistance programs. Others partner with Housing First initiatives, providing wraparound support for people transitioning from homelessness to stable housing.

Practical Pathways: The United States

Policy Reforms Worth Supporting

The Housing Choice Voucher program represents one of America's most effective anti-poverty tools, but funding limitations leave most eligible families without assistance. Expanding voucher funding to serve all eligible households would dramatically reduce housing insecurity. Churches can advocate for this expansion at the federal level while working to improve local implementation and reduce barriers that prevent voucher holders from finding willing landlords.

Zoning reform has gained momentum across the political spectrum. States like California, Oregon, and Minnesota have enacted laws limiting exclusionary zoning practices that restrict multifamily housing. These reforms allow apartments and other affordable housing types in neighborhoods previously reserved for single-family homes.

Churches can support similar reforms in their states, recognizing that resistance to housing construction often reflects the same patterns of exclusion the civil rights movement challenged.

The Low-Income Housing Tax Credit program finances most affordable housing construction in America. Expanding this program and reforming it to serve the lowest-income households better would increase affordable housing supply. Some advocates call for renewed federal investment in public housing or the creation of social housing development authorities modeled on successful international examples. These approaches merit serious consideration given the scale of the shortage.

Tenant protections prevent displacement and provide stability. Rent stabilization policies, just-cause eviction requirements, and the right to counsel in eviction proceedings all help renters remain housed. Churches can advocate for these protections while recognizing the legitimate concerns of small landlords who depend on rental income.

What American Churches Can Do

American churches have a rich history of housing development through faith-based Community Development Corporations. These organizations have built thousands of affordable units while maintaining a connection to congregational values. Churches considering housing development can learn from established CDCs by partnering with experienced organizations or by building internal capacity over time. The Episcopal Church and several mainline Protestant denominations have developed toolkits and support networks for congregations pursuing this path.

Community land trusts offer another model. These organizations hold land in perpetual trust, leasing it to homeowners or developers under conditions that preserve long-term affordability. Churches can contribute property to land trusts, ensuring that their assets serve affordability goals permanently rather than providing a one-time benefit.

Several faith-based land trusts have emerged in recent years, combining community ownership with religious values.

Political engagement through faith-based organizing networks has proven effective on housing issues. Networks like the Industrial Areas Foundation, PICO National Network, and Gamaliel Foundation train congregations in community organizing methods that build power for policy change. These organizations have won significant victories on housing policy in cities and states across the country. Congregations joining these networks gain access to training, resources, and the collective power that comes from acting with allies.

Within their own communities, churches can address the NIMBY attitudes that block housing construction. Many congregants reflexively oppose new housing development near their homes, sometimes on aesthetic grounds, sometimes from concerns about traffic or parking, and sometimes from thinly veiled class or racial prejudice. Pastors and lay leaders can reframe these conversations around values of welcome, justice, and love of neighbor, helping congregants see housing development as consistent with their faith commitments.

Global Perspectives: Lessons for Other Nations

The housing affordability crisis extends far beyond Australia and the United States. Cities across Europe, Asia, and the developing world face similar pressures, though local conditions shape distinct challenges and opportunities. Religious communities in these contexts can draw lessons from the principles outlined above while adapting strategies to their particular circumstances.

The United Kingdom and Ireland

Britain faces a housing emergency rooted in decades of underbuilding and the erosion of social housing. The Right to Buy policy, introduced in the 1980s, allowed council tenants to purchase their homes at significant discounts. While this created wealth for individual families, it depleted the social housing stock without adequate replacement. Today, council housing waiting lists stretch for years, private rents consume unsustainable portions of income in London and other cities, and homeownership has become increasingly confined to those with family wealth.

Irish housing policy followed a similar trajectory, with heavy reliance on private markets and neglect of social provision. Dublin now ranks among Europe's most expensive cities for renters, and homelessness has reached historic highs. Young Irish people face the prospect of permanent exclusion from homeownership in the communities where they grew up.

Churches in Britain and Ireland hold substantial property, particularly the established churches with their historic endowments. The Church of England has begun exploring how its land holdings might serve housing needs, though progress remains slow. Catholic dioceses and other denominations face similar questions about stewardship of assets accumulated over centuries. Advocacy for increased social housing construction, planning reform to enable density, and tenant protections all merit religious engagement. Faith-based housing associations already play significant roles in British social housing provision, offering models that could be expanded.

Western Europe

Germany, France, the Netherlands, and other Western European nations have historically maintained stronger social housing sectors than Anglophone countries. Yet even these systems face pressure. German cities that once offered affordable rents have seen dramatic increases as international capital flows into property markets. The Netherlands struggles with housing shortages despite strong planning traditions. French social housing, though extensive, concentrates poverty in peripheral estates that have become sites of social exclusion.

Religious communities in these contexts operate within different church-state relationships than their Anglophone counterparts. Established churches in Scandinavia and Germany, and the strong

Catholic presence in southern Europe, provide institutional platforms for advocacy. The tradition of Christian Democratic politics in continental Europe has historically supported social housing provision, offering natural allies for faith-based advocacy. Churches can advocate for maintaining and expanding social housing commitments against pressures for privatization and market liberalisation.

East Asia

Hong Kong, Singapore, South Korea, and major Chinese cities face extreme housing affordability challenges. Hong Kong residents endure among the world's smallest living spaces and highest housing costs relative to income. Young Koreans have largely abandoned hope of homeownership in Seoul, coining terms like "hell Joseon" to describe their economic despair. Chinese cities have experienced extraordinary price increases that have enriched property owners while excluding younger generations.

Religious communities in East Asia operate as minorities in largely secular or multi-religious societies. Christian churches, Buddhist temples, and other religious organizations nonetheless maintain significant presence and can contribute to housing solutions. Singapore's public housing model, which houses over eighty percent of the population in government-built flats, demonstrates that Asian societies can achieve housing security through determined policy intervention.[17] Churches can advocate for policies that prioritize housing as shelter over housing as investment, challenging the speculative dynamics that drive unaffordability.

---

[17] Housing and Development Board, Government of Singapore, "Public Housing: A Singapore Icon."

Developing nations face housing challenges of different character and scale. Rapid urbanization has created vast informal settlements lacking secure tenure, adequate services, or safe construction. Slums house over a billion people worldwide, with projections suggesting this number will grow substantially in coming decades. Climate change compounds these challenges, as sea level rise and extreme weather threaten coastal settlements where many of the urban poor live.

Religious communities often maintain their strongest presence precisely in these communities of need. Churches, mosques, and temples in informal settlements provide social infrastructure where government services are absent. Faith-based organizations deliver education, healthcare, and community organization in contexts of extreme deprivation. This presence creates both opportunity and responsibility.

Secure land tenure represents a foundational intervention in many developing contexts. When residents lack legal rights to the land they occupy, they cannot invest in improvements, access formal credit, or resist displacement. Religious organizations can advocate for tenure regularization programs that give informal settlers legal security. Community land trusts, adapted to local legal frameworks, offer models for collective ownership that can protect against both displacement and speculative pressure.

Incremental housing approaches recognize that formal housing standards often exceed what poor households can afford, pushing them into informality. Programs that provide secure tenure and basic infrastructure, allowing families to improve their homes over time, have shown success in various contexts. Religious organizations can support such approaches while advocating for the public investments in water, sanitation, and electricity that make incremental improvement possible.

Microfinance for housing has emerged as a tool for helping low-income households improve their living conditions. Small loans for construction materials, repairs, or incremental additions can significantly improve housing quality when formal mortgage markets are inaccessible. Faith-based microfinance institutions operate in many developing countries and can incorporate housing lending into their portfolios.

Common Principles Across Contexts

Despite vast differences in housing systems, economic conditions, and religious landscapes, certain principles apply broadly.

Housing functions as a foundation for human flourishing everywhere. The theological conviction that every person deserves conditions allowing dignified life transcends cultural boundaries. Religious communities in every context can articulate this vision and work toward its realization.

Market mechanisms alone will not provide adequate affordable housing. Every nation that has achieved broad housing security has done so through significant public intervention, whether through direct provision, regulation, subsidy, or some combination. Religious voices can counter ideological claims that markets will solve housing problems if only freed from interference.

"Every nation that has achieved broad housing security has done so through significant public intervention, whether through direct provision, regulation, subsidy, or some combination. Market mechanisms alone will not provide adequate affordable housing."

Land represents a finite resource with unique characteristics. Its supply cannot be increased in response to demand, and its value derives largely from public investments and community development rather than owner effort. These features justify public intervention to ensure that land serves broad social purposes rather than enriching speculators. Religious traditions that emphasize stewardship over absolute ownership provide resources for articulating this perspective.

Local context shapes effective solutions. What works in Singapore will not work identically in Lagos or London. Religious communities embedded in particular places can discern appropriate strategies while learning from experiences elsewhere. International networks of religious organizations can facilitate this exchange of knowledge and solidarity.

Long-term commitment matters. Housing problems develop over decades and require sustained effort to address. Religious institutions, with their multigenerational perspectives and patient capital, can maintain focus when political attention wanders. This persistence represents one of the church's most valuable contributions to housing work.

The housing crisis is global, and so is the community of faith. Christians in Sydney share communion with Christians in São Paulo, Mumbai, and Manchester. Muslims in Melbourne belong to an ummah spanning continents. This global connection creates both obligation and resource. We are called to care about housing conditions wherever our siblings in faith struggle, and we can learn from their experiences and support their efforts. The work of housing justice, pursued faithfully in diverse contexts, participates in the building of a world where all people can dwell in dignity and peace.

Working Together: Religious and Secular Collaboration

The scale of the housing crisis demands cooperation across traditional boundaries. Religious organizations can partner with government agencies, receiving public funding for service provision while maintaining their distinctive identity. Community housing providers welcome church land contributions and can handle the complex work of development and property management. Secular advocacy organizations benefit from the moral voice and organizing capacity that congregations bring.

Such partnerships require navigating real tensions. Churches entering housing development must maintain transparency and accountability, avoiding the scandals that have occasionally tarnished faith-based social service provision. When accepting government funding, congregations must comply with requirements regarding non-discrimination and the separation of religious programming from publicly funded services. Advocacy coalitions must find common ground across theological differences that participants may hold on other issues.

Despite these challenges, collaboration offers extraordinary potential. Government brings resources and regulatory authority; churches bring land, relationships, and moral legitimacy; nonprofit housing organizations bring technical expertise. When these assets combine effectively, transformative projects become possible. Developments that seemed financially infeasible become viable when donated land reduces costs. Policies that seemed politically impossible gain traction when diverse coalitions of religious and secular voices unite behind them.

The prophetic role of religious communities need not conflict with pragmatic engagement. Churches can work within existing systems to achieve incremental progress while continuing to articulate a vision of justice that transcends current arrangements. The point is to house people, and that goal justifies working with imperfect partners through imperfect processes.

"Our societies need affordable housing, which is a fundamental human right. The prophetic role of religious communities need not conflict with pragmatic engagement. Churches can work within existing systems to achieve incremental progress while continuing to articulate a vision of justice that transcends current arrangements. The point is to house people."

A Call to Action

The moral cost of inaction grows daily. Each year of delay means more families experiencing the trauma of homelessness, more children's development stunted by housing instability, more older adults choosing between medication and rent, more young people locked out of communities where they hope to build their lives. The crisis compounds generationally: children who grow up in housing insecurity face diminished prospects as adults, perpetuating cycles of disadvantage.

Housing serves as a foundation for other goods we value. Educational achievement depends significantly on housing stability, as children who move frequently fall behind academically. Employment outcomes improve when workers can live near jobs without crushing commutes or housing cost burdens. Both physical and mental health correlate strongly with housing security. Family formation and stability require homes where relationships can grow. Religious participation itself depends partly on residential rootedness that allows lasting congregational bonds. When housing fails, these interconnected goods fail with it.

"Housing serves as a foundation for other goods we value. Educational achievement depends on housing stability. Employment outcomes improve when workers can live near jobs. Physical and mental health both correlate strongly with housing security. Family formation requires homes where relationships can grow. When housing fails, these interconnected goods fail with it."

Individual believers can respond in multiple ways. Education comes first: learning about housing policy in your community and understanding the experiences of those facing housing insecurity. Political engagement follows: contacting elected representatives, supporting candidates who prioritize housing, and attending public hearings on development proposals. Financial support matters: contributing to organizations working on housing, whether direct service providers or advocacy groups. Personal relationships count too: opening conversations about housing in your congregation and community, challenging NIMBY sentiments when you encounter them, and welcoming new housing development in your neighborhood.

Congregations can act collectively. Form a housing committee to assess church property assets and explore development possibilities. Join advocacy coalitions working on housing policy. Partner with housing organizations for education and service opportunities. Include housing in your congregation's prayers and preaching. Examine your own attitudes toward housing development and density with honesty and openness to change.

Denominations and religious bodies can coordinate these efforts at scale. Develop toolkits and resources for congregations exploring housing development. Create networks for sharing best practices and lessons learned. Use institutional voice for advocacy at the state and national levels. Examine denominational property holdings for housing potential. Commission theological reflection on housing that grounds practical action in faith tradition.

Home as Holy Ground

The places where we live shape who we become. A child's bedroom becomes the site of imagination and growth. A family's kitchen table hosts conversations that form identity and belonging. A front porch or stoop connects private life to the public community. These ordinary spaces carry extraordinary significance. When they become precarious or disappear entirely, something sacred is lost.

"The places where we live shape who we become. A child's bedroom becomes the site of imagination and growth. A family's kitchen table hosts conversations that form identity and belonging. A front porch connects private life to public community. These ordinary spaces carry extraordinary significance."

Religious traditions have always understood this. The Hebrew word for "dwell" (שכן/shakan) gives us the word for God's indwelling presence among the people, the Shekinah. When we work to ensure that all people have stable, affordable places to dwell, we help create conditions where divine presence can be experienced, and human dignity can flourish.

The housing crisis won't solve itself. Markets left to themselves won't produce the affordable housing that low-income and moderate-income households need. The government alone lacks the resources, legitimacy, and relationships that comprehensive solutions require. Religious communities bring essential elements to this work: theological vision, moral voice, material assets, relational networks, and patient commitment. The question is whether we'll deploy these gifts with the urgency the moment demands.

In Matthew 25, Jesus identifies himself with those in need: the hungry, the thirsty, the stranger, the naked, the sick, the imprisoned.

"Whatever you did for one of the least of these," he says, "you did for me." In our time, the least of these include the mother sleeping in her car with her children, the older man facing eviction, the family paying half their income for a cramped apartment, and the young couple who despair of ever owning a home where they might raise their children. How we respond to them reveals what we truly believe about human dignity, about community, and about the God who chose to dwell among us.

The work is urgent. The resources exist. The question is whether we'll act. Let us build homes, transform policies, and create communities where every person can dwell in dignity and peace.

6. Sitting with Venezuela

I've been sitting with the Venezuela situation, trying to figure out what I actually think. It's one of those cases where I find myself agreeing with people I usually disagree with and disagreeing with people who are typically on my side, which is generally a sign that something genuinely complicated is going on.

So here's where I've landed, for whatever it's worth.

The Part Where the Intervention Seems Defensible

Maduro's government was genuinely awful. I don't think you have to be a Trump supporter to acknowledge this. The UN documented crimes against humanity. The Fact-Finding Mission established by the Human Rights Council found evidence of persecution on political grounds, arbitrary detentions, torture, and sexual violence going back more than a decade. The Bolivarian National Guard was implicated in systematic killings, and the report noted a pattern of structural impunity sustained by a judicial system either unable or unwilling to hold perpetrators accountable. As of late September 2025, Foro Penal counted 827 political prisoners. Nearly eight million people fled the country, generating the largest displacement crisis in Latin American history. Colombia alone absorbed 2.8 million refugees. The 2024 election was stolen in broad daylight, with the regime claiming victory despite voting tallies from more than 80% of polling stations showing opposition candidate Edmundo González won by a two-to-one margin.

María Corina Machado won the Nobel Peace Prize for her nonviolent resistance to this regime. She welcomed the intervention. When someone who spent years risking her life organizing peaceful opposition says "the hour of freedom has arrived," I think that deserves serious weight. It's easy for those of us watching from a comfortable distance to lecture about sovereignty and international norms. She was actually there. She had been living in hiding for fifteen months before escaping to Norway in December to accept her Nobel. On Saturday morning, she issued a letter calling for Edmundo González to assume his constitutional mandate as president immediately.

And there's a tricky question that critics have to answer: what was the alternative? Maduro showed no signs of voluntarily stepping down. Every peaceful avenue had been tried and crushed. The Venezuelan judiciary validated his fraudulent election victory. The government rejected any form of inquiry into the results. Human rights defenders were charged and prosecuted. The staff of the UN human rights office was expelled from the country after reporting on the disappearance of activist Rocío San Miguel. The International Criminal Court had authorized resumption of its investigation into crimes against humanity, but the Venezuelan government stonewalled. Waiting for internal change meant accepting indefinite suffering for millions of people. That's a real cost, even if it doesn't show up in legal briefs about intervention.

The Part That Keeps Bothering Me

Here's my problem. Maduro deserved to be removed, but I was deeply uncomfortable with how it happened and who did it.

The legal issues are real. You can't just dismiss them as anti-Trump bias. International law generally prohibits one country from forcibly removing another country's government, even a terrible one. Article 2(4) of the UN Charter requires sovereign states to refrain from the threat or use of force against the territorial integrity or political independence of another state, with exceptions only for self-defense or Security Council authorization. Venezuela neither launched armed attacks against the U.S. nor possessed the kind of imminent threat that might justify preemptive action under established legal doctrine. The Trump administration invoked anti-drug operations and the 2020 indictments charging Maduro

75

with narco-terrorism, but legal scholars I've read remain skeptical that these provide sufficient grounds for military strikes and the capture of a sitting head of state.

The reasons for that prohibition are compelling when you think about it: who gets to decide which leaders are bad enough to justify invasion? By what standard? The argument that Maduro was exceptionally awful proves too much, because there's no shortage of brutal governments in the world. If American military power becomes the final arbiter of regime legitimacy, exercised whenever a president decides it's warranted, that's a principle with implications far beyond Venezuela.

And then there's Trump himself. His comments about "running Venezuela" and his earlier annexation musings about Greenland, Canada, and the Panama Canal are not subtle. At his Mar-a-Lago press conference on Saturday, he said the U.S. would "run the country" until a "safe, proper and judicious transition" could occur. He declined to commit to any timeline for elections or withdrawal. He dismissed María Corina Machado, saying she "doesn't have the support within or the respect within the country" despite her Nobel Prize and the millions who voted for her candidate. He appeared comfortable with Delcy Rodríguez, Maduro's vice president, potentially taking over, even as Venezuela's Supreme Court directed her to assume presidential duties. These statements suggest Trump understands this intervention in terms that have very little to do with Venezuelan self-determination and a lot to do with American dominance. You can celebrate Maduro's fall while being alarmed about what the person who orchestrated that fall intends to do next. These aren't contradictory positions.

Which brings me to the thing I keep coming back to: we don't actually know yet whether this was a liberation or the beginning of something else. It's January 4th. The capture happened less than 24 hours ago. Will there be free elections? Under Venezuelan law, if the constitutional path is followed, elections should be held within 30 days. Will the U.S. respect the outcome even if Venezuelans choose leaders

Washington doesn't like? Will American forces leave? Trump said he's "not afraid of boots on the ground" and mentioned the U.S. would have "a presence in oil." The answers to those questions will determine whether this looks like a humanitarian intervention or imperial overreach with good PR. Celebrating this as a triumph for freedom before we know the ending feels premature.

The Precedent Problem

This is the part that nags at me most, and I don't see it discussed enough.

For decades, the United States has anchored its moral authority in international affairs on the claim that it supports a rules-based order. When Russia invaded Ukraine, American condemnation rested on the principle that nations cannot simply seize territory or topple governments by force because they find it convenient. When China threatens Taiwan, American warnings invoke the importance of respecting sovereignty and allowing people to determine their own futures.

These principles have always been applied selectively. American foreign policy history is full of coups, interventions, and regime changes that violated the norms Washington simultaneously preached to others. From the CIA-backed coup in Guatemala in 1954 to the 1989 invasion of Panama that captured Manuel Noriega, the U.S. conducted thirteen intervention operations in Latin America during the Cold War alone. Critics have pointed to this hypocrisy for generations. But there's a difference between selective application and open abandonment.

What concerns me about Venezuela is what it signals to other great powers. The message is hard to misread: when a sufficiently powerful nation decides that another country's government is illegitimate or poses a threat to its interests, military force is an acceptable means of resolving the problem. The justifications can vary. Humanitarian concerns. Drug trafficking. Security threats. Protection of co-ethnics abroad. Historical claims. The formula is flexible.

If you're sitting in Beijing, watching the United States remove a government it dislikes in the Western Hemisphere, what lessons do you draw about Taiwan? The U.S. will say the situations are entirely different: Maduro was a dictator, Taiwan is a democracy. But China has its own narrative about Taiwan, one in which reunification is a historical inevitability and American interference is the obstacle to a legitimate resolution. The point is that great powers always have narratives. They always have reasons. The question is whether we want a world where those narratives and reasons, backed by sufficient military force, are all that matters.

Russia already operates this way. The invasion of Ukraine was dressed up in claims about NATO expansion, protecting Russian speakers, and denazification. The international community rightly rejected these justifications as pretexts for imperial aggression. But the rejection carried weight precisely because it appealed to norms that were supposed to be universal. When the United States acts on the principle that it can remove foreign governments it finds objectionable, it becomes harder to articulate why Russia cannot do the same.

I'm not saying these situations are morally equivalent. Maduro was a genuine human rights abuser in ways that the Ukrainian government was not. Taiwan is a functioning democracy, and China has no legitimate claim to govern it. Context matters. Specifics matter.

But international norms gain their power from consistent application. Every exception a great power carves out for itself becomes a template for other great powers to carve out their own exceptions. The rules-based order, already fragile, becomes a polite fiction that everyone invokes when convenient and ignores when inconvenient.

Maybe that's where we already are. Maybe the rules-based order was always more fiction than reality, and the Venezuela intervention is unusually honest about how power actually works. I don't know. But I find myself mourning the principle even as I struggle to condemn its specific application in this case.

The Domestic Constitutional Question

There's another dimension to this that deserves attention: the question of American constitutional law and the separation of powers.

Trump acknowledged at his press conference that he did not notify Congress until after the strike was underway, saying, "Congress tends to leak. It would not be good if they leaked." Democratic lawmakers immediately demanded an immediate briefing and criticized the administration for not seeking congressional authorization. House Minority Leader Hakeem Jeffries said, "Far too many questions remain unanswered." Even Republican Senator Mike Lee of Utah initially questioned whether the U.S. action was constitutional.

The Constitution grants Congress the power to declare war. Over decades, presidents have stretched that constraint through creative interpretations, emergency powers, and the 2001 Authorization for Use of Military Force that was passed initially for Afghanistan but has been invoked to justify operations across the globe. But Venezuela is a new situation. There's no plausible argument that Maduro was connected to the September 11 attacks. There's no treaty obligation at stake. The drug trafficking charges, while serious, don't obviously rise to the level of imminent threat that would justify unilateral executive action.

The question of whether this operation was constitutional was a matter beyond Venezuela. If presidents can launch military strikes, capture foreign heads of state, and occupy countries without congressional approval whenever they invoke drug trafficking or humanitarian concerns, then the war powers clause of the Constitution has been effectively nullified. The legislature becomes an afterthought in decisions of war and peace. This should concern Americans across the political spectrum, regardless of how they feel about Maduro.

On Partisan Epistemology

One correct observation: many of the people criticizing this intervention would have praised the same action if Obama or Biden had done it. I suspect that's true.

But here's the thing. That hypocrisy, if it exists, doesn't tell us whether the intervention was proper. "Your opponents are inconsistent" is a valuable point for scoring political wins and a useless point for figuring out what's actually true. The same applies in reverse, obviously. Plenty of people cheering this on would have called it unconstitutional overreach under a Democratic president.

Would I feel the same way about this if the partisan valence were reversed? I think I would still have the same mix of "Maduro was a monster and his removal is defensible on humanitarian grounds" and "the legal precedent is troubling, and the stated intentions of the administration are alarming." But I'm aware that I might be fooling myself. We're all susceptible to motivated reasoning.

The Regional Response

The reaction from Latin America has been telling. Colombian President Gustavo Petro confirmed multiple strikes in Caracas and condemned the attack as an aggression against Venezuela and Latin America. Brazil's President Lula da Silva said the strikes "crossed an unacceptable line" and set a "dangerous precedent." Mexico's President, Claudia Sheinbaum, invoked Article 2 of the UN Charter. Chile issued a strong condemnation. Cuba's President called it "state terrorism."

These are not Maduro allies speaking. Brazil refused to recognize Maduro's disputed 2024 election victory. Colombia and Mexico have democratic governments with their own concerns about Venezuelan authoritarianism. Yet they're united in condemning the method used to address it. That should give Americans pause. When the entire region, including governments that have no love for Maduro, views American action as a violation of sovereignty and international law, we should at least consider the possibility that they're seeing something we're missing.

The U.N. Security Council is set to meet on Monday on an emergency request from Colombia. The international community is treating this as a serious breach. Whether anything comes of that remains to be seen, given the United States' veto power. But the diplomatic isolation is real, and it carries costs that will outlast this particular operation.

Where I End Up

Genuinely uncertain. And that's okay.

The Maduro regime was a horror. Its end will likely improve the lives of millions of people. The nearly eight million Venezuelans scattered across Latin America and the Caribbean may finally have reason to hope they can return home. The political prisoners may be freed. The torture may stop. That matters enormously.

The method was legally questionable, procedurally concerning, domestically unconstitutional by reasonable interpretation, and carried out by an administration whose vision for Venezuela's future ranges from vague to actively disturbing.

Both things are true. I don't have to pick one. The satisfaction of seeing a dictator fall doesn't require pretending the operation raised no serious concerns. The concerns don't require minimizing the dictator's crimes or the real suffering his government caused.

The following year or two will clarify a lot. If Venezuela gets genuine self-determination, free elections, and American withdrawal, this will look better in hindsight. If we see prolonged occupation, manipulated elections, or resource extraction that benefits American interests while Venezuelans stay poor, the humanitarian framing will look like it was always a pretense.

For now, I'm holding both the hope and the worry. The Venezuelan people deserve freedom. They deserve to choose their own leaders and build their own future. They've suffered enormously, and

81

their suffering deserves to end. Whether this intervention actually delivers that, or replaces one form of external control with another, is a question we can't answer yet.

I'll be watching. We all should be.

PART III: SUFFERING, TECHNOLOGY, AND THE LIMITS OF THE SELF

Part III: Suffering, Technology, and the Limits of the Self confronts what breaks autosanctity open: suffering that resists explanation (Job) and artificial intelligence that challenges human uniqueness.

7. No Easy Answers: What Job Reveals About Suffering, Silence, and the God Who Weeps with Us

"We were promised sufferings. They were part of the program. We were even told, 'Blessed are they that mourn,' and I accept it. I've got nothing that I hadn't bargained for. Of course, it's different when the thing happens to oneself, not to others, and in reality, not imagination." ~ *C.S. Lewis*

Many people's lives are full of suffering. How do we make sense of this suffering? Why does God allow suffering? Why does he allow the innocent and righteous to suffer? Where is God when I'm hurting?

An older man groans in pain, longing for release. A young woman loses her husband in a motorbike accident, leaving her to raise her three children alone. We shudder at the horror of Auschwitz.

We're confronted and offended by such misery. We often search for hidden meaning within suffering itself, or we seek explanations elsewhere.

What Does the Bible Say About Suffering?

The breadth of suffering in the world raises profound questions about the nature of God and his involvement in human life. If God is all good, all-powerful, and all-loving, then why do the innocent suffer?

Neither the Old Testament nor the New Testament provides complete answers to this question. But some answers are given, and these ideas can be explored.

The Bible teaches that we suffer mainly because of the fallen, broken, wounded, and sinful nature of humanity.[18] Sin has entered the world and brought death, disease, division, and destruction. Human beings rebel against God and his holiness, righteousness, and justice. And human bodies and the creation are frail. But, despite this very real struggle, we're assured that God remains King. We're assured that when Christ returns, all things will be eternally restored—and this includes the end of all suffering and evil.[19]

In this life, we experience suffering and pain. These affront our sense of the world's fairness. They raise questions "about the goodness, the compassion, even the existence of God."[20]

Baptist leader Steve Frost has offered insightful reflections on Jesus' parable of the mustard seed.[21] We often misunderstand the parable of the mustard seed. In a world addicted to the shiny, successful, eye-catching, and exponentially growing, the kingdom of God is almost embarrassingly ordinary. But it's perfect for rest, shade, and food. The sun continues to beat down on people, scorching them and causing them to suffer.

The kingdom of God is rest and shade and renewal and hope, but it isn't some giant umbrella that protects us from all pain. But there's hope! Even as the sun beats down, in that very moment, the kingdom of God provides rest, shade, and food. It provides healing, hope, and new life amid pain and suffering. That's the good news.

---

[18] Gen.3.
[19] Col.2:15; cf. 1 Cor.15-54-57; Rev.12:10f.; etc.
[20] Kushner, Harold S. "Why Do the Righteous Suffer? Notes Toward a Theology of Tragedy." *Judaism* 28.3 (Summer 1979): 316. See Kushner, Harold S. *When Bad Things Happen to Good People.* Anchor, 2004.
[21] Matt.13:31–32.

What Does Job Say About Suffering?

The Old Testament book of Job is one source that Christians and Jews turn to for explanations of human suffering and pain. Job is a stunning ancient text. It helps us engage with both the conceptual problems of suffering and the human, interpersonal, gut-level experiences. The misery of innocent, defenseless, and good people is a very real dilemma.

Job is a righteous man who lives a blameless and upright life, fearing God and shunning evil. Despite this, he suffers greatly. He loses livestock, friends, property, health, and his sons and daughters. One calamity is added to the next.

In the story, Job's three friends come to "comfort" him in his suffering. Job's friends believed in a doctrine of divine retribution—a belief that God rewards the righteous and punishes the wicked in this life. But Job questioned this theology when his experience seemed in blatant contradiction to its proposals and convictions.

Why do some people embrace the doctrine of divine retribution to explain pain and suffering? There are several motivations behind this approach. Some adopt it as a way to understand and control their circumstances while protecting God's image as both omnipotent and good. Others hold to this doctrine to preserve religious and theological traditions. Still others use it as an ethical or moral motivation for righteous living.

However, the results of this doctrine can be deeply problematic. It often leads to the condemnation of fellow human beings who are suffering. The sufferer themselves is forced to blame themselves for their circumstances. Perhaps most troublingly, God is reduced to an adversary rather than a source of comfort. Ultimately, no satisfactory answer is provided for the person who is actually experiencing the suffering.

When the Righteous and Innocent Suffer

The book of Job denies the doctrine of divine retribution. Job's friends hold rigidly to the doctrine of divine retribution and encourage Job to repent. They say that if he repents, he'll escape his suffering and receive God's blessing. In doing so, they "unsuspectingly tempt him to use God for his personal gain, [which is] the essence of sin."[22] If Job had followed their counsel, he would have vindicated his accusers, who claimed that human beings seek personal gain in their worship of God. Using the words of the three "comforters", the author of Job "strongly denounces the practice of using deceptive arguments to defend God."[23]

The book of Job offers no definitive answer to the problem of human misery.

The issue is ventilated, and Job's friends offer partial answers. But, in the end, "readers can't discover from the book any one clear view about what the reason for their own particular suffering may be, nor any statement about the reason for human suffering in general; for the book is entirely about the suffering of one particular and unique individual."[24]

The book of Job doesn't deny that sufferers sometimes deserve suffering. Yet, it contradicts the idea that this is always the case. Job exemplifies the innocent sufferer, whose innocence is asserted by the story's narrator, the holy God, and himself.

The book of Job tells us that the righteous and innocent may suffer terribly, and that adverse circumstances don't necessarily witness to an individual's moral corruption. Righteous and innocent people may suffer deeply in every sphere of life (physical, social, spiritual, and emotional).

---

[22] Hartley, J.E. *The Book of Job: The New International Commentary.* Eerdmans, 1988. p. 48.
[23] *Ibid.* p. 49.
[24] Clines, D.J. "Job" in *Word Biblical Commentary.* Word, 1989, p. xxxviii.

Forget Those Clever Answers to the Meaning of Suffering

Job doesn't portray the suffering of the righteous, innocent, and good as something that's necessarily cleansing, educational, testing, or edifying. The author upholds the goodness of both God and Job. But human will, the laws of nature, human sin, and the brokenness of the world all combine to contribute to the suffering of the innocent, exculpating God and the sufferer from responsibility.

Yet even these "clever" explanations don't heal the wounds nor satisfy the objections of the millions who are suffering. There is no clear answer to the question of human suffering in the book of Job.

The mistake of Job's friends was that they offered complicated explanations to an innocent sufferer who, in fact, needed comfort, support, and sympathy. He didn't need their clichéd or "clever" answers.

We learn from Job that God isn't predictable, and it's completely acceptable to question God when we're in pain. But no thorough explanation of human misery is provided, nor attempted in the book.

The problem of suffering (as distinct from the experience of suffering) is a problem for the monotheist only. Only the monotheist asks, "How can the one true God be omnipotent, good, and compassionate when the innocent and righteous suffer?" A polytheistic, pantheistic, or atheistic view of the world doesn't need to ask such a question. For the monotheist, misery has a moral or ethical quality attached to it. It's seen as wrong, unjust, and in need of reconciliation with our understanding of the one good God.

But the book of Job, to the frustration of many monotheists, isn't a theodicy. A theodicy is an attempt to justify the ways of God to human beings (or an attempt to vindicate divine providence in the face of evil and suffering). Theodicies strive to resolve the problem of evil and suffering for a theological system. They seek to demonstrate that God is omnipotent, all-loving, and just—despite the existence of misery and evil.

Job, however, is primarily the personal account of one man's unique experiences of suffering.

The book is about his wrestle with the meaning of human misery. It's far removed from the Augustinian theodicy (the free will defense), the Irenaean theodicy (the soul-building theodicy incorporating a consequentialist ethic), or the Leibnizian theodicy (the best of all possible worlds theodicy). It's not a theodicy, because Job doesn't attempt to explain the problem of suffering and evil.

At the same time, Job rejects the doctrine of corruption (everything suffers because everything is corrupt). And it rejects the stoic idea that we're required to transcend our misfortunes in this life and receive our reward in the next.

Tilley was correct when he wrote that the book of Job "displays the cost of providing the 'systematic totalization' a theodicy requires: silencing the voice of the sufferer, even if s/he curses the day s/he was born and accuses God of causing human suffering."[25]

In the book of Job, theodicies are at best represented by the impetuous young Elihu, who is full of hot air. Or, at worst, they're "not quite torturers, but all the forms of intimidation, all the psychological conditionings, are good for them to obtain the famous spontaneous confessions so dear to dictatorial societies."[26] The book of Job develops no coherent theodicy. It provides no theological foundations for establishing a modern theodicy. That isn't the purpose of this ancient drama.

---

[25] Tilley, T.W. "God and the Silencing of Job", in *Modern Theology*, 5, April 1989, p. 267.
[26] *Ibid.*

It's OK to Question God

In the book, Job is never condemned for questioning God. In desperate anguish, he gropes for answers in the dark abyss of his misery. He laments his bitter feelings and grievous calamities. He cries to God for a response.

Job questions God vigorously—not logically or consistently, but in one motivated by grief and inner turmoil. "Job thus legitimates for sincere believers their ambiguous feelings toward God and religion when they suffer intensely for no discernible reason."[27]

Job is convinced that he's become a mockery to his neighbor. He knows that, although he is blameless, he is a laughing stock, while "the tents of robbers are prosperous, and those who provoke God are secure."[28] He is sure that the beasts, birds, reptiles, and fish will testify that God is to blame for his calamity: "Which of all these doesn't know that the hand of God has done this? In his hand is the soul of every living thing, and the life breath of all humankind."[29]

Job exclaims that God negates the expectations of the religious establishment. God makes fools of judges; silences trusted advisers, and takes discretion away from the aged. Job, based on this evidence, concludes: "I want to speak with the Almighty; I wish to reason with God."[30] God then allows Job to question him unashamedly, forthrightly, and openly.

God is more offended by unauthentic piety or dogmatic orthodoxy than by those who love him and who ask him direct questions—including questions about the meaning of their misery. God doesn't require that we repress our anger or grief. He doesn't require us to settle for petty or trite answers about the nature, meaning, and origins of evil and suffering.

---

[27] Lella, A.D. "An Existential Interpretation of Job", in *Biblical Theology*, 15, April 1985, p. 51.
[28] Job 12:8.
[29] Job 12:7–10.
[30] Job 13:3.

The book of Job legitimates "the quest of believers for self-understanding and meaning, while at the same time encouraging them to display emotional integrity and candor in their relationships with God and others. It also validates their moments of skepticism in the face of commonly accepted certainties as well as pessimism as a frank response to an implacable experience, and perhaps even cynicism in reaction to unmerited abuse from others."[31]

Once Job has aired his criticisms and questions of God, he encounters God's majesty and is overwhelmed that God would even reason with him. In his encounter with God, he finds profound personal meaning, amidst undeserved suffering and ambiguity. God responded to Job's cries of anguish in this encounter. This is because the author of the book of Job believes that God responds to human misery—sometimes incomprehensibly, often unfathomably, but never negligibly.

God responds to Job's questioning. But he doesn't do it in a manner that would silence through fear, persuade by love, placate with logical explanations, or bribe to keep Job silent. Instead, God responds in the divine-human encounter, allowing Job to glimpse the respective places of God and human beings in the universe.

The book tells us that God permits evil and chaos for a season, but that they're kept on a leash.

In the face of suffering and injustice, human beings have the responsibility to pursue and display morality, compassion, justice, freedom, and hope. No concise theodicy is given in the book, however, since such theologically rigid constructs won't constrain God.

The book of Job is scathing of Job's friends, and their easy, clever, and clichéd answers to the problem of evil and suffering. Job shows us that when people suffer, we should listen to them compassionately rather than offer clichéd answers that don't address their pain. We also learn to trust in the goodness of God to work everything out in the end.

---

[31] Lella, A.D. *Op.Cit.* 55.

The message of the book is that there's no rigid answer to these difficult questions, and it's acceptable to question God. We don't have to settle for superficial answers to the problem of suffering and evil. Life is full of contradictions and pain. The righteous and innocent sufferer may find hope and peace in trusting God, even if they can't find satisfactory answers to their painful questions.

So, Where is God When it Hurts?

The question remains: if God takes pleasure in us, then why do the innocent suffer?

Here are some responses.

But keep in mind what has been written above about the unsatisfactory nature of simplistic answers when we, or someone we love, is experiencing suffering.

God Suffers

The Bible shows us a God who isn't distant from human suffering. God himself suffers. And he suffers greatly.

Jesus experienced profound suffering: physical (from hunger, weariness, flogging, and crucifixion), emotional (he wept for Lazarus and grieved for the fall of his people), and mental and spiritual (such as his agony in the garden and his torment on the Cross).

Jesus identifies with innocent sufferers because he himself was an innocent sufferer.

Paul describes Christ as our intercessor in heaven who deeply understands, shares, and experiences our sufferings—because he himself has suffered. God himself is a suffering God. He's the "crucified God." God won't know the end of his pain and heartbreak over our suffering until the restoration of all things through Christ (i.e., the second coming). We aren't alone in our pain, for when we suffer, he suffers with us.

God is Present in Our Suffering (and Suffering Shapes Us)

Since God is involved in our suffering, he can work through it for our good (even though suffering is never good in itself).

Since God's presence is with us when we suffer, he may *use* suffering to draw us to Christ, develop in us Christian maturity, and accomplish his purposes. (Note that I've said he does not *cause* suffering for his people. It's still a terrifying thought, though—God *uses* pain to bring us to him).[32]

As C.S. Lewis once famously wrote, "God whispers to us in our pleasures, speaks in our conscience, but shouts in our pain: it's His megaphone to rouse a deaf world."[33]

C.S. Lewis says that suffering can lead us to humility and to a dependence on God. (But suffering can also lead us to final and unrepentant rebellion). Suffering can also break down our wrong ideas about God. Suffering can (but doesn't always) lead to hope. And suffering only makes sense in the light of the final chapter—the new heaven and new earth in Jesus Christ.

It's essential, then, to reflect on our response to suffering.

A first response is to ask ourselves some questions. We might begin by asking whether this suffering is a result of our own sin or lifestyle, and if so, what we should change. It's worth noting that while the answer here may sometimes be yes, it is often no—frequently it is the righteous and innocent who suffer most. We should also ask whether God is trying to speak to us in the midst of this suffering, not necessarily causing it but communicating something to us through it.

Once we've asked those questions, there are several things we can do. However, I recognize how difficult some of these actions are, especially when we're experiencing physical pain and emotional anguish. We can hold on to the promise that God is with us in our suffering and cling to the hope of eternal healing. We can show others compassion in

---

[32] See Heb.5:8; 1 Peter 1:7.
[33] Lewis, C.S. *The Problem of Pain*. HarperCollins, 1996. p. 91.

their suffering and refuse to offer sufferers simplistic or clichéd answers. We might also resist suffering through medical intervention and pray for healing, which may or may not come through prayer, depending on God's will. Where appropriate, we can change our lifestyles and habits and minister to those who suffer.

Finally, we should remember the Cross, the Resurrection, and Christ's Return. The Cross shows us that God suffers and shares our pain, revealing the incredible suffering of Christ to redeem and restore the world. The Resurrection witnesses to new life and new creation in Jesus Christ, as well as to the resurrection of our whole, healed, and restored bodies. Christ's Return gives us hope for the new heaven and earth at the end of the age, established through the rule and reign of Jesus Christ.

God Takes Pleasure in Us

The Bible teaches us that God takes pleasure in his children. He delights in us. The reality of suffering doesn't change that.

It's this delight in us that caused Christ to endure the suffering of the Cross, and that causes God to be both a "suffering God" and a "crucified God." He offers us eternal freedom from pain and suffering, even though we often suffer greatly in this lifetime. He is present with us in our suffering. He brings comfort, hope, loving friends, and, sometimes, but not always, even physical healing.

God Gives Us Hope

The New Testament brings an entirely new perspective to our understanding of suffering: the perspective of eternity. Paul wrote, "The sufferings of this present time aren't worthy to be compared with the glory that will be revealed in us."[34]

We suffer in this life. Faith doesn't protect us from that. Indeed, we're promised suffering if we follow Christ.

---

[34] Rom.8:18.

But the Bible says that we can hope in the new heaven and the new earth, where there will be no more pain or suffering. This life is as a drop in the ocean compared with our eternal peace, joy, and wholeness with God. Such thoughts don't always comfort us when we suffer, or when we've lost someone we love. But, at times, such hope does help make the suffering of this life more bearable—and direct our hearts and minds to our eternal hope in Jesus Christ.

The meaning of human misery will perplex us for as long as suffering exists. Why does suffering exist? What is its origin or cause? Why am I personally suffering? Why do the righteous and innocent suffer if God is just, all-powerful, and all-loving? What is the meaning of human misery?

I began with the book of Job, and I'd like to return there. Job legitimates our natural tendency to question God when undeserved calamity strikes.

The message of the book of Job is that there's no rigid answer to these difficult questions. And it's acceptable to question God. We don't have to settle for superficial answers to the problem of suffering and evil. Life is full of ambiguities, paradoxes, and uncertainties. Yet, somehow, in the midst of this chaos, God works out his purposes—bringing hope, healing, peace, and new life.

The righteous and innocent sufferer may find hope and peace in trusting God, if not answers to their painful questions. The Christian God is a "crucified God." He is a "suffering God." He takes pleasure in us, and he's present with us in our suffering. The Christian God has suffered and continues to suffer.

But he is also the "resurrected and returning God," who offers the hope of the new creation and the restoration of all things. His glory will be revealed in us.

Suffering only makes sense in the light of the final chapter—the restoration of all things, at the end of the age, in Jesus Christ. You and I will be suffering in this life. But, "the sufferings of this present time aren't worthy to be compared with the glory that will be revealed in us."[35]

[35] Rom.8:18.

8. The Breath and the Algorithm: A Christian Theological Response to Artificial Intelligence

Something unprecedented is happening, and the church is largely silent.

Not silent in the way we're sometimes silent before mystery, that pregnant, worshipful hush that precedes genuine encounter with the Holy. No, this is a different kind of silence. It's the silence of confusion. Of overwhelm. Of a community uncertain how to speak a theological word into a moment that feels both utterly new and strangely ancient.

Artificial intelligence is now woven into the fabric of daily existence. It curates the news we read, shapes the diagnoses our physicians consider, determines who receives loans and who is flagged as a security risk, and writes code, poetry, and legal briefs. Large language models can now pass professional licensing examinations, engage in nuanced philosophical debate, and generate images of such verisimilitude that the distinction between captured reality and synthesized fiction has become functionally meaningless for most observers. Autonomous systems make decisions with consequences that ripple across economies, ecosystems, and individual lives.

And here we stand, followers of the One who spoke the cosmos into being, who breathed life into dust, who took on flesh and dwelt among us, uncertain whether we have anything distinctive to say.

We do. We must.

The Temptation of Technological Totalism

The dominant narrative around artificial intelligence oscillates between breathless utopianism and apocalyptic dread. On one side, prophets of technological salvation promise that superintelligent machines will solve climate change, cure cancer, eliminate poverty, and usher humanity into a post-scarcity paradise. On the other hand, doomsayers warn of existential catastrophe, systems that escape human control, economic displacement on a civilization-ending scale, and the reduction of human beings to obsolete relics of biological history.

Both narratives share a common feature that should immediately alert the theologically attentive: they're fundamentally eschatological. They traffic in ultimacy. They position artificial intelligence as either savior or destroyer, as the hinge upon which the human story will turn. They invite us to place our hope, or our fear, in machines.

"The threat isn't that AI will replace us. The threat is that we'll forget who we are."

This is the old temptation in new garments. The tower of Babel was also a technology project, an attempt to secure human destiny through human ingenuity, to build a structure that would reach the heavens and make a name for its builders. The golden calf was a technology, a manufactured object onto which ultimate trust was transferred. The empires that have risen and fallen throughout history have each believed themselves to be the culmination of progress, the final word.

The Christian tradition has always known that technologies, like all created things, are neither neutral nor ultimate. They aren't neutral because they shape us even as we shape them. The medium is never merely instrumental; it forms habits of attention, patterns of relationship, assumptions about what matters and what is possible.[36] And they aren't ultimate because the arc of history bends not toward algorithmic

---

[36] This insight is indebted to McLuhan, *Understanding Media.*

optimization. Still, toward the reconciliation of all things in Christ, a hope that no machine can deliver and no machine can thwart.

Our first theological task, then, is to name this moment rightly: neither to baptize the hype nor to succumb to the panic. We're witnessing a genuinely significant technological transition, one that will reshape labor, communication, creativity, and warfare in ways we can't yet fully anticipate. But we aren't witnessing the arrival of a new god. We aren't standing at the edge of redemption or annihilation by silicon. We're living through a chapter in the ongoing human story, a story that remains, as it has always been, under the sovereign care of the One who was and is and is to come.

Image-Bearers in an Age of Intelligent Machines

The question of what it means to be human has never been more urgent.

For centuries, theologians and philosophers have defined human distinctiveness in terms of capacities: reason, language, creativity, moral agency, and consciousness. We're the beings who think, who speak, who create, who choose, who are aware of ourselves being aware. These capacities were understood as reflections of the divine image, marks of the Creator's imprint upon creatures uniquely formed for relationship with the Holy One.

Artificial intelligence doesn't simply challenge this framework; it renders it philosophically precarious. Large language models generate text that is grammatically coherent, contextually appropriate, and at times genuinely insightful. Image generators produce art that evokes an emotional response. Game-playing systems develop strategies no human has conceived. If human distinctiveness rests on these functional capacities, what happens when machines replicate them?

Some will respond by moving the goalposts, insisting that machines don't really understand, don't really create, don't really feel. There is something to this response. The computational processes that generate large language model outputs aren't phenomenologically equivalent to human thought. There is no evidence of subjective experience in these systems, no inner theatre of meaning-making. They're, in a technical sense, very sophisticated pattern-matching engines.

But this defense, while not without merit, misses the deeper theological point. The Christian tradition has never finally grounded human dignity in capacities, not in reason, not in language, not in creativity, not in consciousness. It has grounded human dignity in relationship. We're made in the image of God, and this imaging isn't primarily about what we can do but about whom we're made for. We're the creatures addressed by name, called into covenant, invited into communion.[37] Our capacities don't earn our dignity; it's bestowed by the One who knew us before we were formed in the womb.

"The image of God is a relationship to be received and enjoyed."

This is liberating news. It means that human beings who can't reason at high levels, infants, those with profound cognitive disabilities, and people at the end stages of dementia are no less image-bearers than those at the peak of intellectual capacity. And it means that machines, however sophisticated their outputs, don't become image-bearers by mimicking human functions. The image of God isn't a feature to be replicated; it's a relationship to be received.

Yet we must be careful not to become triumphalist here. The fact that machines can't become image-bearers doesn't mean their development poses no challenge to human flourishing. The opposite may be true. If we reduce ourselves to our functional capacities, if we allow economic systems, social structures, and cultural narratives to define human worth by productivity and cognitive performance, then we'll have already surrendered the very understanding of humanity that protects us. The threat isn't that AI will replace us. The danger is that we'll forget who we are.

---

[37] For theological anthropology grounding the *imago Dei* in relationality rather than capacities, see Barth, *Church Dogmatics* III/2; and more recently, Kelsey, *Eccentric Existence*.

The Attention Economy and the Formation of Souls

Here's where the pastoral dimension becomes urgent.

Long before large language models captured public imagination, machine learning systems were already reshaping human consciousness through social media algorithms, recommendation engines, and targeted advertising. These systems are optimized to capture and hold attention, and they're extraordinarily effective. The average person now spends multiple hours daily in digitally mediated environments designed by some of the most sophisticated engineering teams in history to maximize engagement.

"Attention is the currency of the soul. What we attend to, we become, and what or Who we worship, we reflect."

The consequences for spiritual formation are profound. Attention isn't a neutral resource to be allocated; it's the currency of the soul. What we attend to, we become.[38] The spiritual masters of every tradition have known this: that prayer is fundamentally a discipline of attention, that contemplation is learning to see, that the distracted mind is incapable of deep formation. When our attention is constantly fragmented, pulled toward novelty, controversy, and superficial stimulation, we become fragmented people, anxious, reactive, unable to sustain the patient presence that love requires.

The church has always understood that formation happens through practice. We become who we are through what we do repeatedly. The liturgical rhythms of worship, the disciplines of prayer and fasting, the habits of hospitality and service, these aren't arbitrary religious requirements but the very means by which Christ is formed in us. When algorithmic systems train us in different habits, the habit of scrolling, of outrage, of curated self-presentation, of constant comparison, they're forming us into different kinds of people.

---

[38] On attention and spiritual formation, see Weil, *Waiting for God*; and Smith, *Desiring the Kingdom*.

This isn't a call to technological withdrawal. The Amish option isn't available to most of us, nor is it necessarily faithful. We're called to be present to our moment, to engage the world as it is, to bear witness in the midst of whatever cultural currents we find ourselves navigating. But engagement mustn't mean capitulation. The church needs to develop robust practices of digital wisdom, not as a set of rules about screen time but as a spirituality of attention in an age of distraction.

What might this look like? It might look like recovering the practice of Sabbath, not merely as a day off but as a countercultural declaration that our lives aren't defined by productivity, that we aren't always available, that the world can turn without us for twenty-four hours. It might look like learning to pray with our phones in another room, reclaiming the silent spaces where the still small voice can be heard. It might look like building communities where we encounter one another in the full complexity of embodied presence rather than through the flattening lens of social media profiles.

Justice and the Algorithmic Order

But personal spiritual practices, vital as they are, can't be the whole of our response. The God of Scripture is a God of justice, and the prophetic tradition demands that we attend not only to the formation of individual souls but to the shape of social structures. Here, too, artificial intelligence poses challenges that require theological engagement.

Consider the question of algorithmic bias. Machine learning systems are trained on historical data, which reflects historical injustices. When these systems are deployed to make consequential decisions about hiring, lending, medical treatment, and criminal sentencing, they can perpetuate and amplify existing inequities. Studies have documented that facial recognition systems perform significantly worse on darker-skinned faces; that recidivism prediction algorithms reinforce racialized patterns in the criminal justice system; and that hiring algorithms replicate the demographic imbalances of past workforces.[39]

The technical response to these problems is essential: better data, more diverse training sets, algorithmic audits, and fairness constraints. But the theological question cuts deeper. These systems encode particular assumptions about what counts as risk, qualification, and success. They operationalize definitions of human flourishing that may be radically at odds with the kingdom of God. When an algorithm defines the ideal job candidate by reference to the characteristics of past successful employees, it enshrines as objective truth what may be the accumulated prejudice of human gatekeepers.

The prophetic tradition teaches us to be suspicious of systems that claim neutrality while reinforcing the advantage of the already-advantaged. It teaches us to ask: Who benefits from this arrangement? Whose voices were not included in its design? What assumptions about human worth and social ordering are embedded in its logic? These aren't merely technical questions to be resolved by engineers. They're questions of justice that demand the engagement of communities formed by the memory of liberation, by the story of a God who hears the cry of the oppressed.

The church has work to do here, not primarily as technology experts (though some of us may be) but as bearers of a different imagination. We have a story to tell about human dignity that isn't reducible to algorithmic inputs and outputs. We have practices of discernment that attend to the stranger, the marginal, the easily overlooked. We have a prophetic mandate to speak truth to power, even when power speaks in the neutral-seeming language of optimization and efficiency.

---

[39] See Buolamwini and Gebru, "Gender Shades"; and Noble, *Algorithms of Oppression.*

Truth, Trust, and the Epistemological Crisis

We're living through an epistemological crisis, a crisis of knowing and believing.

The capacity to generate synthetic media, images, audio, and video that appear authentic but are entirely fabricated represents a qualitative shift in the information environment. We're approaching a threshold beyond which seeing will no longer be believing, where any piece of evidence can be plausibly claimed to be fake, where the default posture toward information becomes suspicion. The implications for democratic discourse, for journalism, for the possibility of shared truth are severe.

But the crisis of truth isn't primarily technological. It's spiritual. Long before deepfakes, we had become a people for whom truth was instrumental, a tool to be deployed in service of other ends rather than a good to be sought for its own sake. Post-truth culture did not begin with AI; it started with the slow erosion of practices and communities oriented toward truth-telling.

The Christian tradition has resources here. We follow one who declared, "I'm the way, the truth, and the life." Truth, in this proclamation, isn't merely propositional; it's personal. It's encountered in a relationship. And this suggests that the restoration of truth-telling can't be accomplished by technological fixes alone, better fact-checking algorithms, or more reliable authentication systems, critical as these may be. It requires the recovery of communities oriented toward truthfulness as a way of life.

The church, at its best, is such a community. It's a place where confession is practiced, where we name our failures honestly rather than constructing flattering narratives. It's a place where we commit ourselves to speaking the truth in love, even when truth is costly. It's a place where we learn to trust one another through long fidelity, through the slow work of keeping promises over time. These practices won't solve the deepfake problem. But they may cultivate in us the kind of truthful character that can navigate an age of epistemic uncertainty without descending into nihilism or paranoia.

Work, Vocation, and the Coming Disruption

The economic implications of artificial intelligence are impossible to predict with precision. Some analysts project massive displacement as automation extends beyond routine manual tasks into cognitive and creative domains. Others anticipate new forms of work emerging, as they have in previous technological transitions. Both outcomes may prove true in different sectors and at different speeds.

What is clear is that the meaning of human work is at stake. For many people, work isn't merely a source of income; it's a source of identity, dignity, social connection, and purpose. The Protestant tradition elevated work to a vocation, a calling through which we participate in God's creative and sustaining activity in the world.[40] When that vocation is threatened or eliminated, the wound isn't only economic but existential.

The Christian response can't be to baptize the coming disruption as progress or to resist it as demonic. It must involve deeper theological reflection on the relationship between human dignity and human work. The Sabbath command reminds us that our productivity doesn't define us, that rest, not labor, is the goal toward which creation moves. The feeding of the five thousand and the vision of manna in the wilderness suggest a God who provides abundantly, outside the calculus of merit and exchange. These texts don't offer an economic programme. But they de-center work from the place of ultimate significance, creating space for a more expansive understanding of human flourishing.

If significant displacement does occur, the church will need to be a place where people can find belonging and purpose outside the structures of paid employment. This isn't a new challenge; the church has always ministered to those at the margins of economic systems. But

---

[40] On vocation and work, see especially Volf, *Work in the Spirit*.

the scale may be new, and our imagination will need to expand accordingly.

Witness in the Age of Intelligent Machines

What, finally, is the posture of Christian witness in this moment?

It's a posture of engaged hope. Not optimism, optimism is cheap, and the challenges ahead are real. But hope: the conviction that history isn't careening toward meaningless chaos or algorithmic control but is held in the hands of a faithful God who is making all things new. This hope doesn't make us passive. It frees us to engage without desperation, to act without the illusion that everything depends on us, to work for justice and wisdom, knowing that the final word has already been spoken.

It's a posture of humble wisdom. We don't have all the answers. The technical complexities are real, the ethical dilemmas are genuine, and the future is uncertain. But we have a tradition of moral reflection, a community of discernment. This story teaches us to attend to the vulnerable and to be suspicious of the claims of the powerful. We bring these resources to the conversation not as experts in machine learning but as participants in the long human struggle to live faithfully before God.

It's a posture of embodied presence. In an age of increasing virtualization, the church continues to gather people in physical space, to share bread and wine, to lay hands on the sick and dying, to baptize with water, to embrace the grieving. This embodied practice isn't a quaint relic; it's a prophetic witness to the incarnational heart of Christian faith. God did not send an algorithm. God became flesh. And the communities that bear witness to this scandalous particularity have something essential to offer a world increasingly mediated by screens.

It's a posture of patient formation. Quick fixes or clever strategies won't meet the challenges of this moment. They require the slow cultivation of wisdom, the long obedience in the same direction, and the daily practices of attention, prayer, and love that shape us into people capable of faithful discernment. The church has been forming people for two thousand years. This work continues.

We aren't the first generation to face disorienting technological change, and we won't be the last. But we're the generation called to bear witness in this particular moment, to name the idolatries of our age, to protect the dignity of those whom economic systems would discard, to tell the truth when lies proliferate, to gather communities of formation when attention fragments, to hold open the space of hope when despair beckons.

"The breath came before the algorithm. The Word was spoken before the code was written."

The breath came before the algorithm. The Word was spoken before the code was written. And when all the systems have run their course, when the servers cool and the data centers fall silent, the love that called the cosmos into being will still be singing over creation, making all things new.

This is our hope. This is our witness. This is the word we have to speak.

PART IV: THE SELF THAT RESTS

Part IV: The Self That Rests offers the theological alternative: the Incarnation as the answer to the exhausted sacred self (Christmas), and embodied solidarity in the face of tragedy (Bondi).

9. Christmas and the Hope of the World: The Light of Christ That Enters Everything

I remember, as a boy, the magic of Christmas morning: waking before dawn, creeping down the hallway, heart pounding with anticipation at what waited beneath the tree. The lights, the tinsel, the smell of my mother's cooking, the rustling of wrapping paper: it all shimmered with a wonder I couldn't name. I remember those special occasions when my parents would take us to Christmas celebrations at the Sydney Opera House, and how marvelous the whole Christmas experience seemed. But as I grew, something more profound began to stir beneath the excitement. Sitting in candlelit church services, singing carols whose words I was only beginning to understand, I sensed that Christmas was reaching for something far larger than gifts and gatherings.

The story of a baby born in the night, of shepherds and angels, of a star blazing over Bethlehem: it wasn't just beautiful. It was cosmic. Slowly, stumblingly, I began to realize that this strange and tender story was the hinge of history, the moment when heaven tore open, and hope took on flesh. The wonder I'd felt as a child wasn't something to outgrow; it was something to grow into. For the mystery at the heart of Christmas, I would come to learn, is nothing less than the hope of the world.

"The wonder I'd felt as a child was something sacred to grow into."

The Light of Christ That Enters Everything

There's a peculiar quality to the darkness just before dawn. It seems thicker somehow, more resolute, as if the night knows its reign is ending and so presses harder against the coming light. We live, in so many ways, in just such a darkness. The crises that encircle our world (ecological collapse, technological disruption, war, hunger, despair) press upon us with a weight that can feel insurmountable. We have built systems that devour the earth. We have constructed economies that crush people with low incomes. We have invented tools whose power outpaces our wisdom. And in honest moments, we wonder whether hope itself has become a luxury we can no longer afford.

Into this darkness, Christmas speaks, not with the voice of easy optimism or shallow sentiment, but with something far stranger and more subversive: the proclamation that the Infinite has become intimate, that the Creator has entered creation not as conqueror but as infant, not in power but in poverty, not to escape our condition but to share it utterly.

This is the mystery at the heart of the Christian celebration of Christmas (the Incarnation), and it's precisely this mystery that speaks with prophetic urgency into the fractures of our contemporary world. The theological meanings of Christmas aren't archaic doctrines to be preserved under glass; they're living realities that judge, heal, and transform. They offer not solutions in the technical sense but something more essential: a reorientation of our seeing, a conversion of our imagining, a new possibility for being human in a world that's forgotten what humanity is for.

"The Incarnation announces that God has married Godself to creation permanently, irrevocably, and that this union is the engine of a transformation that won't rest until all things are made new."

For Christians, this isn't merely poetic language or metaphorical comfort. It's an ontological claim. In Christ, something has happened to the very structure of reality. The Light that shines in the darkness is

110

salvation: a rescue operation launched from the heart of God into the depths of human captivity. The One born in Bethlehem comes not only to show us the way but to be the way, not only to speak truth but to embody it, not only to point toward life but to become, in that fragile infant flesh, the very life of the world.

This is the staggering scope of Christmas: that in this child, God has begun the work of gathering up all that is broken, all that is lost, all that groans under the weight of sin and death, and weaving it back into wholeness. Nothing lies beyond the reach of this redemption: not the desecrated earth, not the ravaged psyche, not the war-torn nation, not the soul that has given up on itself. The Incarnation announces that God has married Godself to creation permanently, irrevocably, and that this union is the engine of a transformation that won't rest until all things are made new. Christmas is the declaration that the cosmos has a future, that despair isn't the most profound truth, and that the darkness, however thick it seems in these final hours before dawn, has already been penetrated by a Light it can never overcome.

Israel-Palestine: The Land Where It Began

There's a weight to the fact that we can't speak of Christmas without speaking of that particular land: the hills of Judea, the town of Bethlehem, the region we now call Israel and Palestine. The Incarnation didn't occur in some generic spiritual space. God entered history at a specific latitude and longitude, among a particular people, in a place that remains to this day contested, bloodied, and broken. This is unbearably significant.

The child born in Bethlehem was Jewish. This must be said clearly and without embarrassment, for the history of Christianity is stained by the horror of forgetting it. Jesus was circumcised on the eighth day according to the law of Moses. Jesus learned Torah at the feet of Jewish teachers. Jesus prayed Jewish prayers, observed Jewish festivals, and lived and died as a faithful son of Israel. The salvation Christians proclaim comes, as the Scriptures insist, from the Jews.

Any Christianity that forgets this (that allows itself to be infected by the ancient poison of antisemitism) has betrayed not only the Jewish people but the Jewish Messiah it claims to worship. The resurgence of antisemitism across the globe, the desecration of synagogues, the targeting of Jewish communities (including recently in Bondi in my home city, Sydney), the casual hatred that's found new life in digital spaces: all of this stands under the absolute judgment of the One who was born King of the Jews. There can be no equivocation here. To hate Jewish people is to hate the people of Jesus. It's a sin that strikes at the very heart of the Christmas mystery.

"To hate Jewish people is to hate the people of Jesus, and to hate Jesus himself. It's a sin that strikes at the very heart of the Christmas mystery."

And yet the land of Christ's birth is also home to another people: Palestinians who have lived on that soil for generations, who have their own history, their own identity, their own legitimate aspirations, and their own profound suffering. Palestinian Christians trace their faith to the earliest Christian community. These Palestinian Christians are "living stones" in the Holy Land. Palestinian Muslims and Christians alike have experienced displacement, occupation, loss, and grief that cry out for acknowledgment and response.

The violence that's engulfed this land (the terror attacks that have murdered Israeli civilians, the military operations that have devastated Palestinian communities, the long grinding weight of occupation, the rockets, the bombs, the children dead in their beds) all of it's a wound in the body of the world. And it's a wound located precisely where the Prince of Peace drew first breath.

How do we hold this? How do we speak of Christmas hope in the shadow of such suffering?

We begin, perhaps, with lament. The tradition of biblical faith knows that some realities are too heavy for explanation, too terrible for premature resolution. They can only be carried into the presence of God and wept over. The psalms of lament, the tears of the prophets, the cry of dereliction from the cross: these are the language we need when words of comfort come too cheaply. We must let our hearts be broken by what breaks the heart of God.

But, if it's honest, lament opens onto something else: the recognition of shared humanity. Israeli parents and Palestinian parents both weep the same tears over the bodies of their children. Both Israelis and Palestinians know the taste of fear, the pain of loss, the desperate longing for a future that isn't defined by violence. The God who became human in Christ became human without qualification: not Israeli or Palestinian, not Jew or Gentile only, but flesh and blood in its universal vulnerability.

This doesn't mean that all claims are equal or that justice is irrelevant. It means that no people, no nation, no cause is entitled to dehumanize the other. The moment we begin to speak of any group as less than fully human (as deserving of collective punishment, as reducible to the worst actions of their members), we have departed from the vision of the Incarnation, which insists that every human being bears the image of the One who chose to bear our image in return.

Christmas calls us to the agonizing discipline of dual compassion: compassion that refuses the false comfort of choosing sides in a way that allows us to stop seeing. It asks us to hold in our hearts the Israeli family shattered by a terrorist's attack *and* the Palestinian family buried beneath the rubble of their home. Not as a political calculus, not as a both-sides equivalence that ignores context and power, but as a spiritual practice of refusing to let any of God's children become invisible.

This isn't a solution. There are no easy solutions, and anyone who claims otherwise is selling something. The political and historical complexities of this conflict exceed the grasp of any single perspective. What is needed (negotiations, agreements, compromises, justice, security) lies beyond what any blog post or sermon can provide.

But Christmas does offer something essential: a vision of what peace means and what it costs. The peace proclaimed by angels isn't the peace of exhaustion, where one side has been beaten into submission. Isn't the peace of forgetting, where history is erased for the sake of

113

moving on. It's the peace of reconciliation: a peace that requires truth-telling about the past, justice in the present, and the unimaginable grace of enemies learning to see one another as kin.

Such peace is impossible. It's as impossible as a virgin birth, as impossible as God in a manger, as impossible as love stronger than death. And yet the entire Christian faith is founded on the conviction that the impossible has happened and continues to happen wherever human beings open themselves to the in-breaking of divine grace.

The land where Jesus was born deserves such grace. Its peoples (all its peoples) deserve a future not defined by the trauma of the past. The stones of Bethlehem, over which tourists walk to visit the site of the Nativity, are the same stones that have witnessed centuries of conquest and suffering. They wait, as all creation waits, for the redemption that the child born among them came to bring.

This Christmas, we must pray for the peace of Jerusalem, and the peace of Gaza, and the peace of Tel Aviv, and the peace of the West Bank, and the peace of every village and city in that wounded land. We must pray with the honesty to confess that we don't know what such peace would look like in practice. We must pray with humility, acknowledging our own complicity in systems of violence and injustice. We must pray with the courage to resist the antisemitism that desecrates the memory of Jesus's own people and the dehumanization that renders Palestinian suffering invisible.

And we must let our prayer become action: advocacy, generosity, presence, solidarity with those on every side who work for peace at high personal cost. For the hope of Christmas is a hope that took on flesh and walked into the world. It asks us to do the same.

The child of Bethlehem grew up to weep over Jerusalem, longing to gather its children as a hen gathers her brood under her wings. That longing has not ceased. It echoes through the centuries, through the violence, through the failure of every peace process and the collapse of every ceasefire. It waits for people willing to be gathered: willing to set down the weapons of fear and take up the vulnerability of trust.

May such people emerge. May we be part of their emergence.

And may the land where hope was born become, at last, a place where hope can live.

Economic Inequality: The Humility That Judges Our Power

Consider the strange economics of the Christmas story. The Divine doesn't arrive in Rome, the seat of empire, nor in the halls of religious authority, but in a backwater province, to an unmarried peasant, in a shelter for animals. The birth is attended not by dignitaries but by shepherds: workers of the night shift, inhabitants of the margins, people whose testimony was legally worthless. This is revelation.

In a world racked by economic inequality and the brutal mathematics of wealth concentration, where billions struggle for daily bread. In contrast, others accumulate resources beyond imagination; the manner of Christ's coming pronounces judgment and offers invitation. The judgment is this: every system that exalts the powerful and discards the vulnerable stands under divine critique. The God who chose a manger has no interest in our pyramids of privilege.

But there's also an invitation: a call to discover that true abundance lies not in accumulation but in self-giving, not in securing our own position but in descending, as God descended, into solidarity with those who have nothing. The Christmas mystery suggests that the path to genuine human flourishing runs directly through the places we have been trained to avoid.

Mental Health and Loneliness Crisis: Emmanuel in the Age of Isolation

The name given to the child is Emmanuel, God with us. Not God above us, directing from a safe distance. Not God against us, threatening from the heavens. With us. Present. Near. Intimate.

We inhabit a world in the grip of a mental health crisis so pervasive that loneliness itself has become epidemic. Despite (or perhaps because of) our ceaseless connectivity, we're more isolated than ever. The technologies that promised to bring us together have often pulled us apart, leaving us scrolling through curated images of lives we don't live, comparing ourselves to phantoms, aching with a nameless hunger that no algorithm can satisfy.

Into this ache, the Incarnation speaks a word of presence. The fundamental promise of Christmas is that we aren't alone: not in our suffering, not in our confusion, not in the depths of our night. The Divine has chosen to be present with us in flesh and blood, in vulnerability and limitation, in all the mess and beauty of embodied existence. This presence doesn't solve our problems in any straightforward way, but it does something perhaps more important: it tells us that presence itself (being with and for one another) is the shape of divine love.

The crisis of mental health is, at its root, a crisis of disconnection. The Christmas proclamation insists that reconnection is possible, that isolation isn't the final word, that the One who made us for communion has entered our solitude to lead us back toward one another.

Ecological Destruction: Light in the Darkness of Ecological Collapse

The poetry of Christmas is saturated with images of light. A star blazing in the eastern sky. Angels illuminating shepherds' fields. The prophetic announcement that those who walked in darkness have seen a great light.

We need such light now. The earth groans under the weight of our consumption. Species vanish before we have learned their names. The climate shifts, and with it, the stability of systems upon which all life depends. We have treated creation as a warehouse rather than a sanctuary, as a resource rather than a gift, and now the consequences of our blindness accumulate with terrible momentum.

The Incarnation offers a radical revaluation. If God has entered matter, if the Word has become flesh, then the material world isn't merely the backdrop for the spiritual drama but part of the drama itself. Creation isn't something to be escaped or exploited but honored and tended. The

116

birth of Christ sanctifies embodied existence in all its forms: the soil, the water, the creatures, the intricate web of relationships that constitute the community of life.

To take the Incarnation seriously is to recognize that ecological destruction isn't merely a policy failure but a theological crisis: a failure to perceive the sacred presence that pulses through all things. Christmas calls us back to reverence, to the recovery of what ancient traditions called *sacramental vision*: the capacity to see in every creature, every landscape, every ecosystem a word spoken by the One whose entry into creation has dignified creation beyond measure.

Geopolitical Instability and Armed Conflict: Peace in a World at War

The angels sang of peace. This is perhaps the most haunting dimension of the Christmas proclamation, for it stands in such stark contrast to our persistent reality. Wars proliferate. Conflicts frozen for decades have thawed into fresh violence. Nations arm themselves with weapons capable of ending civilization itself. The dream of peace seems naïve at best, delusional at worst.

And yet the Christmas message isn't naïve. It doesn't pretend that peace is easy or inevitable. The child whose birth the angels announced would grow to speak of peace in disturbing terms: not as the world gives, but as something more profound, more complex, more demanding. The peace of Christ isn't the absence of conflict but the presence of justice, not the mere cessation of violence but the reconciliation of enemies, not the victory of one side but the transformation of all.

This peace is eschatological: it belongs to God's promised future. But it's also, mysteriously, present wherever communities embody the reconciling love revealed in the Incarnation. Christmas reminds us that peace isn't simply a political achievement to be engineered but a spiritual reality to be received and practiced. It begins not in treaties but in transformed hearts, in the daily discipline of forgiveness, in the costly refusal to return evil for evil.

In a world of geopolitical instability, the Christmas peace is both judgment and possibility. It judges every ideology that makes violence sacred, every nationalism that dehumanizes the other, every calculation that treats human beings as acceptable losses. And it holds open the possibility that another way of being together (difficult, demanding, but real) has been inaugurated in the birth of the Prince of Peace.

Artificial Intelligence: The Wisdom We Need for the Technology We Have Created

Among the most pressing challenges of our moment is the governance of artificial intelligence: a technology of immense power whose implications we're only beginning to glimpse. We have created minds that aren't minds, intelligences without wisdom, capabilities without conscience. And we're uncertain how to proceed.

The Christmas story offers no direct guidance on algorithmic ethics. But it does offer something essential: a vision of what wisdom looks like. The God who becomes human in Christ demonstrates that true power is always in service of love, that knowledge divorced from compassion is dangerous, and that the measure of any capacity is whether it serves the flourishing of all.

"True power is always in service of love . . . knowledge divorced from compassion is dangerous."

The Incarnation is, in a sense, the original act of divine self-limitation. The Infinite accepts the constraints of finitude. The All-Powerful embraces vulnerability. This self-limiting love stands as a profound challenge to our technological moment, which tends to celebrate power without limit, capability without constraint, growth without boundary.

What would it mean to approach our most powerful technologies with something of the humility modelled in the Christmas mystery? What would it mean to ask not simply "What can we do?" but "What ought we to do, and for whose benefit, and at what cost?"

Food and Water Security: Bread for the World's Hunger

The child was born in Bethlehem: a name that means "house of bread." This is the kind of detail that rewards contemplation. Food security remains elusive for hundreds of millions of people. Supply chains strain under the pressure of climate disruption and conflict. The specter of famine haunts regions already traumatized by poverty and war.

The One born in the house of bread would later take bread, bless it, break it, and give it away, declaring it to be a sign of divine presence and self-gift. The Eucharistic tradition that flows from this action insists that bread is never merely bread, that the material realities of food and sustenance are caught up in the purposes of God.

Christmas reminds us that God's concern is utterly concrete. The Incarnation isn't an abstraction but flesh and blood, hunger and thirst, the body's need for nourishment. A faith formed by the Incarnation can't be indifferent to the empty bellies of the world's children. It must be a faith that feeds, that shares, that organizes its common life around the conviction that no one should go hungry while others feast.

Democratic Erosion and Misinformation: Truth in an Age of Deception

We live in an era when the very concept of truth is contested. Misinformation spreads faster than fact. Institutions that once served as arbiters of reliability have been compromised or discredited. Democratic discourse, which depends on some shared commitment to truthfulness, erodes under the acid of cynicism and manipulation.

The Fourth Gospel calls Christ the Word (the *Logos*), a term freighted with philosophical meaning. It suggests that in Christ, the rational structure of reality, the truth at the heart of all things, has become visible and personal. The one who would later say "I am the truth" enters the world as a defenseless child, demonstrating that truth isn't a weapon to be wielded but a gift to be embodied.

119

The Christmas proclamation challenges both the cynics who deny that truth exists and the ideologues who claim to possess it absolutely. It suggests that truth is ultimately personal, relational, and self-giving, and that this truth can only be approached with humility, received with gratitude, and shared with love.

In a world drowning in propaganda and lies, the church's vocation is to be a community of truthfulness: not in the sense of having all the answers, but in the sense of being committed to honest speech, careful thinking, and the hard work of discernment that genuine truth-telling requires.

Biodiversity Crisis: The Renewal of All Things

The biodiversity crisis is, in its deepest dimension, a crisis of imagination. We have lost the capacity to see other creatures as fellow participants in the drama of existence, fellow recipients of divine attention and care. The extinction of species proceeds unnoticed mainly because we have ceased to notice the more-than-human world at all.

But the Christmas story is populated with animals. Tradition places ox and donkey at the manger. Shepherds bring the memory of their flocks. The natural world isn't merely scenery but a participant.

The Incarnation announces that God's redemptive purpose embraces all creation. The birth of Christ inaugurates a new creation: not the replacement of the material world with something purely spiritual, but the renewal and restoration of all that exists. Every species, every ecosystem, every intricate relationship within the web of life falls within the scope of God's saving intention.

This is a theological claim with practical implications. If the birth of Christ signals the renewal of all things, then the destruction of any thing (any species, any habitat, any irreplaceable fragment of the community of life) is a wound to the body of creation that Christ came to heal.

The Hope That Isn't Optimism

We must be clear: the hope of Christmas isn't optimism. Optimism is a temperament, a prediction about outcomes, a calculation of probabilities. The hope announced in the Incarnation is something else entirely. It's a theological virtue: a gift of the Spirit that enables us to live toward a future that isn't yet visible, to act in faith when the evidence is against us, to persist in love when love seems futile.

This hope doesn't deny the darkness. It doesn't pretend that the crises facing our world are illusory or easily solved. It knows that the child born in Bethlehem would grow to be executed by the empire, that the path of incarnate love leads through suffering and death.

But it also knows that death didn't have the last word. And so it dares to believe that death won't have the last word in the crises of our own time: not over the earth, not over the poor, not over the victims of war, not over the lonely and despairing, not over the truth, not over any creature beloved by the One who came among us.

"The hope of Christmas isn't optimism . . . It's a theological virtue: a gift of the Spirit that enables us to live toward a future that isn't yet visible."

This is hope anchored not in circumstance but in the character of God: the God who specializes in bringing life from death, who called light out of primordial chaos and called Lazarus out of the tomb. Christian hope is resurrection hope: the unshakeable conviction that the same power that raised Christ from the grave is at work in the world still, bending the arc of history toward redemption, refusing to abandon what's been made and loved.

Christmas is the annual renewal of this hope. It's the church's stubborn insistence, year after year, in the teeth of all evidence to the contrary, that the light shines in the darkness and the darkness has not overcome it.

May we receive this hope. May we embody this hope. May we become, in our small and faltering ways, bearers of this hope to a world that desperately needs it.

For the hope of Christmas is nothing less than the hope of the world.

10. We're One Australian People: A Christian Reflection After Bondi

These have been heavy days.

Our Jewish neighbors are mourning the loss of loved ones and wondering if they're safe. Our Muslim neighbors grieve alongside them while bracing for the suspicion and hostility that so often follows. And all of us, whatever our background, are wrestling with the kind of violence that shakes something loose in the soul.

On a recent Sunday, Bondi Beach should've been alive with the joy of Hanukkah: families gathering, candles lit, a community celebrating light in the darkness. Instead, it became the site of Australia's worst mass shooting in nearly three decades. Fifteen lives were taken: a ten-year-old girl named Matilda; an eighty-seven-year-old man who had survived the Holocaust only to die in an act of antisemitic terror; two beloved rabbis; a couple who gave their lives trying to wrestle a weapon from one of the killers. Dozens more carry wounds, visible and invisible. A community has been torn open.

For those of us who seek to follow the Way of Jesus, moments like this strip away all pretense. We can't retreat into comfortable theology or partisan point-scoring. We are confronted, again, with the question that lies at the heart of discipleship: "What does God's love and discipleship to Jesus require of us now?"

It's natural to want answers: someone to blame, some failure of policy or leadership that, if only corrected, would've prevented this. And there'll be a time for those hard questions; accountability matters. But I want to suggest that right now, the deeper call is toward one another.

We've frightened neighbors. We've communities wondering whether they truly belong in this country. We've a fragile social fabric that could tear further, or could hold.

Australia, at its best, has shown a remarkable capacity to bridge differences and find common ground. That capacity isn't automatic; it's a choice, made again and again, especially when it's costly. As Christians, we believe we've been shown a Way: not a way of fear or vengeance, but of self-giving love, even for those we find most challenging to love. This is the moment to walk that Way together.

What Does Faith Ask of Us Now?

As a Christian, I find myself turning to the witness of Jesus in moments like this, not for easy answers, but for orientation. What does faithfulness look like when the ground beneath us feels so unsteady?

First, I think it looks like grief. The Psalms of lament teach us that honest sorrow before God isn't a failure of faith but an expression of it. Jesus himself wept. We don't need to rush past the horror of what happened, or smooth it over with platitudes. We can sit with our Jewish neighbors in their pain, bearing witness, simply being present. Sometimes there are no adequate words, and that's alright.

Second, it looks like solidarity. Jesus was Jewish. The Hebrew scriptures are Christian scripture. An attack on Jewish people celebrating a festival of liberation isn't someone else's tragedy; it's an assault on those to whom Christians are spiritually indebted. Standing with the Jewish community isn't optional for those who follow Jesus; it flows from the very logic of our faith.

Third, it looks like refusing to let fear and hatred have the last word. The attackers wanted to fracture us, to turn communities against one another, to make us retreat into suspicion and tribalism. The resurrection is, among other things, a declaration that violence and death don't write the final chapter. Christians are called to be people who live by that hope, who continue to build bridges across difference, even when it's costly.

Grace for Each Other

Our politicians are human beings navigating something genuinely difficult: trying to condemn violence without inflaming hatred, trying to protect some of us without alienating others. They won't get it perfectly right. None of us would.

It's also painfully easy, in moments of grief and fear, to lash out: to attack those we already disagreed with, to score points against the other side, to let ethnic or political or religious divisions sharpen into weapons. But when we do this, we only throw fuel on the fire. We become part of the problem we claim to oppose. And we fail to reflect the reconciling, peacemaking Messiah who blessed the peacemakers and called his followers to be agents of reconciliation in a fractured world.

What I'd love to see in the coming days is something that's become rare: a little grace. For each other. Even for those we disagree with. Not because accountability doesn't matter, but because we're more likely to find our way through this together than we're tearing strips off one another.

This doesn't mean ignoring hard truths. Any honest Christian reckoning must acknowledge the long, shameful history of Christian antisemitism, from medieval pogroms to the complicity of churches in the Holocaust to the conspiracy theories that still circulate in some corners today. Repentance is an ongoing posture. If hatred has found any foothold in our own communities, this is the moment to root it out.

And we must hold space, too, for Muslim Australians who are grieving this tragedy while fearing what may come next. The perpetrators claimed an ideology that the vast majority of Muslims find abhorrent. To punish a whole community for the actions of murderers would be to compound one injustice with another. That isn't the way of Jesus, who consistently reached across the boundaries his society had drawn.

The Harder Work of Consistent Truth-Telling

There's a temptation, in moments like this, to speak only the truths that come easily to our side. But if we believe that truth-telling is an act of love, and as Christians, we should, then it can't be selective. It has to cut across all our tribal loyalties.

So let me say plainly what needs to be said: antisemitism has been allowed to fester in Australia, and the failure to name it clearly and confront it consistently is part of how we got here. When Jewish students feel unsafe on university campuses, when synagogues require armed guards, when "Zionist" becomes a slur hurled at anyone who is visibly Jewish, these aren't abstractions. They're the soil in which violence grows. We can't claim to be shocked by the harvest if we've tolerated the sowing.

This deserves to be said. Jesus himself was willing to speak hard truths, even uncomfortable ones. Matthew 23 shows us a Messiah who didn't shy away from naming what was wrong, even when it cost him. Prophetic speech is part of faithful discipleship.

But here's the question I find myself asking: have we been consistent truth-tellers ourselves? Have we spoken up about antisemitism with the same energy we've brought to other causes, or only when it's been politically convenient? And have we also spoken up about Islamophobia, about the deaths of tens of thousands of civilians in Gaza, about the suffering of Palestinians under occupation, about Indigenous suffering in our own backyard, and about the rise of aggressive nationalism among young men in our country?

Or do we only tell the truth when it suits our ideological tribe?

This isn't whataboutism. It's a question about integrity. If our moral voice is selective, fierce about the injustices committed by those we already oppose, silent about those committed by our allies, then we've forfeited our prophetic authority. We've become partisans with a religious veneer, and the world can smell the hypocrisy from a mile away.

The same Jesus who excoriated the Pharisees also wept over Jerusalem. The same Lord who overturned tables in the temple touched lepers and spoke tenderly with Samaritans. Truth and grace weren't opposites for him; they were integrated. He could hold the complexity because his vision wasn't tribal; it was shaped by the coming Kingdom, where every victim matters and every perpetrator is called to account.

So yes, let's tell the truth about the antisemitism that has been tolerated for too long in progressive spaces, on campuses, and in public discourse. Let's name it for what it is: an ancient hatred that has repeatedly erupted in mass murder, and which must be confronted with the same moral seriousness we bring to any other form of racism.

And let's also be honest with ourselves. Have we wept for the children of Gaza as readily as we weep for the children of Bondi? Have we named the dehumanization of Palestinians with the same clarity we bring to the dehumanization of Jews? Have we noticed the young men in our own congregations being radicalized by online ideologies of resentment and supremacy?

The Christian calling isn't to pick a side in the culture war; it's to bear witness to a Kingdom that judges all our kingdoms. That means we'll sometimes be out of step with everyone. Our progressive friends may be frustrated when we insist on naming antisemitism they'd prefer to ignore. Our conservative friends may be frustrated when we insist on naming injustices they'd prefer to excuse. So be it. Faithfulness to Christ has never been a path to popularity.

What I'm calling for isn't neutrality; neutrality in the face of evil is its own kind of failure. I'm calling for consistency: a willingness to apply the same moral standards to all parties, to grieve all victims, to hold all perpetrators accountable, and to refuse the easy tribalism that sees atrocities only when committed by the other side.

This is hard. It requires us to hold multiple truths at once: that this attack was a horrific act of antisemitic terror, and that Palestinian civilians are also dying in unconscionable numbers. That Muslim Australians deserve protection from bigotry, and that Islamist extremism is a genuine

127

threat that must be confronted. That our political opponents are often wrong, and that they are also made in the image of God.

The world doesn't need more Christians who function as chaplains to one political tribe or another. It needs followers of Jesus who can hold complexity, who can weep with all who weep, who can speak uncomfortable truths to every side, and who can model the kind of moral consistency that points beyond our fractured politics to the reconciling love of God.

We need to examine our hearts and our speech. As Christians, our truth-telling can't afford to be partisan. If we're going to insist that truth-telling is an act of love, and we should, then it has to apply even when the truth implicates us and our allies. That's the more complex work. And it's the work to which Christ calls us.

Light in the Darkness

Amid the horror, there were also glimpses of extraordinary courage. Boris and Sofia Gurman, a Russian-Jewish couple, tried to disarm one of the attackers and were killed in the attempt. Ahmed al-Ahmed, a Syrian-born fruit shop owner, wrestled a gun away from one of the shooters. Lifeguards rushed into danger with surfboards as stretchers. In the days since, a record number of Australians have signed up to donate blood.

This is who we are at our best. Not the violence, but the response to it. Not the hatred, but the hands reaching out across every divide to help.

The Prime Minister asked Australians to put candles in their windows, a reminder that light can defeat darkness. For Jews celebrating Hanukkah, the festival of lights, this image carries particular resonance. For Christians approaching Christmas, it echoes our own conviction that no darkness is so deep that it can't be overcome.

We're one Australian people. That's not naive, it's a choice we make, again and again, especially when it's hard. It's a choice to see in our neighbors, whoever they are, the image of God. It's a choice to build a society where everyone can celebrate their faith without fear.

Let's make that choice now.

May the God of all comfort be with those who mourn. May we have the courage to be peacemakers. And may the light not be overcome.

Light That Can't Be Overcome: A Prayer After Bondi

God of all comfort and God of all peoples,
      you who scattered the proud in the imagination of their hearts
      and lifted up the lowly,
      you who sent your Son to be light in the darkness,
      a light no darkness has ever overcome,
      we come to you in this hour of grief and fear.

You're the God who chose Abraham and Sarah,
      who liberated Israel from Egypt,
      who sent prophets to call your people back,
      who in the fullness of time became flesh in a Jewish child
      born to a Jewish mother,
      raised in the rhythms of Torah and Temple.
The scriptures of Israel are our scriptures.
The story of the Jewish people is integrated into our story.
An attack on your ancient people is an assault
      on those to whom we're forever spiritually indebted.

You're the God who weeps with those who weep,
      who numbers every hair on our heads,
      who sees every victim,
      who remembers every name.

We confess, O Lord, with heavy hearts and bowed heads,
      the long, shameful history of Christian antisemitism.
From medieval pogroms to centuries of persecution,
      from the complicity of churches in the Holocaust
      to the conspiracy theories that still circulate in our midst,
      we've sinned against our elder siblings in faith.
We've twisted your scriptures to justify hatred.
We've blamed your chosen people for the death of your Son,
      forgetting that he laid down his life freely,
      that Roman and Jew and Gentile and all humanity
      stand equally in need of grace.

We confess that antisemitism has been allowed to fester
      in our society, in our institutions, in our discourse.
We've watched Jewish students feel unsafe on campuses.
We've grown accustomed to synagogues needing armed guards.
We've heard "Zionist" become a slur
      hurled at anyone visibly Jewish,
      and too often we've been silent.
We can't claim to be shocked by this harvest
      when we've tolerated the sowing.

We confess, too, our selective truth-telling.
We've spoken up only when it suited our tribe.
We've been fierce about injustices committed by those we oppose
      and silent about those committed by our allies.
We've become partisans with a religious veneer,
      and the world has smelled our hypocrisy.
We've failed to weep with all who weep,
      to grieve all victims,
      to hold all perpetrators to account.
Forgive us, Lord, and restore to us
      the integrity of prophetic witness.

We lament, O God, the horror of what has happened.
Bondi Beach should have been alive with the joy of Hanukkah:
       families gathering, candles lit,
       a community celebrating light in the darkness.
Instead, it became a site of mass murder,
       the worst in this land in nearly thirty years.

We weep for Matilda, only ten years old.
We weep for the eighty-seven-year-old man
       who survived the Holocaust
       only to die in an act of antisemitic terror.
We weep for the two beloved rabbis,
       for Boris and Sofia Gurman,
       the couple who gave their lives
       trying to wrestle a weapon from the killers.
We weep for the fifteen whose lives were stolen,
       for the dozens who carry wounds visible and invisible,
       for a community torn open.

We grieve with our Jewish neighbors
       who mourn their dead and wonder if they are safe.
We grieve with our Muslim neighbors
       who share in this sorrow
       while bracing for the suspicion and hostility
       that so often follows.
We mourn the ancient hatred that keeps erupting,
       the tribalism that tears communities apart,
       the ideologies of resentment and supremacy
       that radicalize young men into murderers.

How long, O Lord?

How long until your people can worship without fear?

How long until festivals of light

        aren't interrupted by the darkness of violence?

How long until we learn to see in every neighbor

        the image of God?

Yet even in this darkness, O Lord, we turn to you in hope.

For we've seen glimpses of extraordinary courage:

        Boris and Sofia, who gave their lives to protect others.

        Ahmed al-Ahmed, a Syrian-born fruit shop owner,

        who wrestled a gun from one of the shooters.

Lifeguards who rushed into danger with surfboards as stretchers.

Record numbers who signed up to donate blood.

This is who we are at our best:

        not the violence, but the response to it;

        not the hatred, but the hands reaching out

        across every divide to help.

We remember that Jesus himself wept.

He wept over Jerusalem,

        he wept at the tomb of Lazarus,

        he carries our sorrows still.

The same Lord who overturned tables in the temple

        touched lepers and spoke tenderly with Samaritans.

Truth and grace were not opposites for him;

        they were integrated.

He could hold the complexity

        because his vision was not tribal

        but shaped by the coming Kingdom,

        where every victim matters

        and every perpetrator is called to account.

We remember the resurrection:

>your declaration that violence and death
>
>isn't write the final chapter.

The light shines in the darkness,

>and the darkness has not overcome it.

Even now, you're at work:

>bringing comfort to those who mourn,
>
>drawing together communities that could have fractured,
>
>kindling candles in windows across the nation.

So we come to you now with our petitions, O Lord.

Comfort those who mourn.

Be near to the brokenhearted.

Hold the families who'll face empty chairs

>at every gathering from now on.

Heal those who carry wounds in body and soul.

Give rest to the traumatized,

>peace to the terrified,
>
>hope to those who feel the ground beneath them is unsteady.

Give us courage to name antisemitism

>clearly and confront it consistently.

Help us see it for what it is:

>an ancient hatred that has repeatedly erupted in mass murder,
>
>a poison that must be confronted
>
>with the same moral seriousness we bring to any racism.

Root it out wherever it has found foothold:

>in progressive spaces and conservative ones,
>
>on campuses and in congregations,
>
>in public discourse and private hearts.

And give us the integrity to be consistent truth-tellers.
Help us weep for the children of Bondi
      and for the children of Gaza.
Help us name the dehumanization of Jews
      and the dehumanization of Palestinians.
Help us confront Islamist extremism
      while protecting Muslim Australians from bigotry.
Help us notice the young men being radicalized
      by online ideologies of resentment and supremacy.
Free us from partisan blinders
      that see atrocities only when committed by the other side.

Give wisdom to our leaders.
They're navigating something genuinely difficult:
      trying to condemn violence without inflaming hatred,
      trying to protect some without alienating others.
Grant them grace when they stumble,
      and grant us grace for them.

Protect our Muslim neighbors
      from the backlash that so often follows.
The perpetrators claimed an ideology
      that the vast majority of Muslims find abhorrent.
To punish a whole community for the actions of murderers
      would be to compound one injustice with another.
That isn't the way of Jesus,
      who consistently reached across
         the boundaries his society had drawn.

And so we commit ourselves, O Lord,
      to walking the Way of Jesus in this moment.

We commit to grief:

> to sitting with our Jewish neighbors in their pain,
>
> bearing witness, being present,
>
> not rushing past the horror with platitudes.

We commit to solidarity:

> standing with the Jewish community
>
> not as an optional act of kindness
>
> but as an expression of the very logic of our faith.
>
> Jesus was Jewish.

The Hebrew scriptures are Christian scripture.

An attack on Jewish people celebrating liberation

> isn't someone else's tragedy; it's ours.

We commit to refusing fear and hatred the last word.

The attackers wanted to fracture us,

> to turn communities against one another,
>
> to make us retreat into suspicion and tribalism.

We won't give them that victory.

We'll continue to build bridges across difference,

> even when it's costly.

We commit to grace for one another:

> for our political opponents,
>
> for those we disagree with,
>
> for leaders who won't get it perfectly right.

We won't lash out in grief,

> score points against the other side,
>
> or throw fuel on the fire we claim to oppose.

We commit to repentance:

        an ongoing posture, not a single moment.

If hatred has found any foothold in our communities,

        we'll root it out.

If our truth-telling has been selective,

        we'll expand our vision.

If we've been chaplains to one political tribe,

        we'll learn again to bear witness

           to a Kingdom that judges all our kingdoms.

We commit to being one Australian people.

This is our choice,

        made again and again, especially when it's hard.

It's a choice to see in our neighbors, whoever they are,

        the image of God.

It's a choice to build a society

        where everyone can celebrate their faith without fear.

Until the day when swords are beaten into plowshares

        and nations learn war no more;

        until the day when the wolf lies down with the lamb

        and nothing hurts or destroys on all your holy mountain;

        until the day when every tear is wiped away

        and death is swallowed up in victory;

        until the day when your Kingdom comes in fullness

        and your will is done on earth as it is in heaven,

Keep us faithful.

Keep us hopeful.

Keep us together.

Keep us reaching across every divide

with hands that help rather than harm.

Keep us lighting candles in our windows,

refusing to let darkness have the final word.

Blessed are you, God of Abraham, Isaac, and Jacob,

who chose a people to be a blessing to all nations.

Blessed are you, Christ who wept over Jerusalem,

who died outside the city gate,

who rose to reconcile all things.

Blessed are you, Spirit who broods over chaos,

who brings order from disorder,

who makes of scattered peoples one new humanity.

May the God of all comfort be with those who mourn.

May we've the courage to be peacemakers.

And may the light not be overcome.

Amen.

Epilogue: The Self That Learns to Rest

The self is still weary. The screens still glow. The notifications still pulse their small demands for attention. The platforms still promise recognition, the markets still offer identity for purchase, the culture wars still rage with their rival sanctimonies. Nothing seems to have changed.

And yet, for those who have learned to see, everything is different.

The same exhaustion that once felt like personal failure now reveals itself as the predictable consequence of bearing a weight the self was never designed to carry. The same conflicts that once seemed like battles between good and evil now appear as collisions between rival autosanctities, each defending its sacred ground with righteous fury. The same restlessness that once drove the endless scroll now becomes an invitation: a longing that points beyond itself toward the rest it can't manufacture.

Diagnosis is a form of liberation. When we name what ails us, we begin to loosen its grip. Autosanctity thrives in darkness, in the unexamined assumption that the self must be its own ground, its own meaning, its own god. Brought into the light, the assumption reveals its absurdity. The self that makes itself a god will discover the misery of its divinity. The temple is too small. The worshiper and the worshiped are the same, and this identity is exhausting. No one can sustain it forever.

"The collapse is into arms that are waiting. Giving up is the beginning of receiving."

The invitation that stands against autosanctity is the invitation to be held. The self doesn't have to hold itself together. It can be received, known, and named from beyond itself. It can rest in an identity it did not construct. The collapse is into arms that are waiting. Giving up is the beginning of receiving. The letting go is how one discovers that one was held all along.

This isn't a technique or a strategy. It's closer to a surrender, and surrender can't be achieved; it can only be allowed. The self that has spent years constructing, performing, defending, and demanding recognition doesn't simply decide one morning to stop. The habits run too deep. The reflexes are too ingrained. The platforms keep pulsing. The culture keeps pressing. Something from outside the self must break in.

Grace is the word for that breaking in. It arrives unbidden, often unwanted, always unearned. It comes in the voice of a friend who sees through the performance and loves anyway. It comes in the suffering that strips away every pretense, leaving only the naked self before God. It comes in the strange silence of a Tech Sabbath, when the noise finally stops and something deeper begins to speak. It comes in the words of Scripture, ancient and foreign, that somehow name what we couldn't name ourselves. It comes in the bread and the wine, the water and the oil, the gathered community that holds us when we can no longer hold ourselves.

Grace comes, above all, in the Incarnation: the announcement that God has entered the world, that the sacred isn't elsewhere, that the One who spoke the cosmos into being has taken on flesh and dwelt among us. Christmas is the annual renewal of this impossible news. The self doesn't have to construct its own meaning, because meaning has been given. The self doesn't have to achieve its own worth because worth has been declared. The self doesn't have to bear the weight of ultimacy, because the Ultimate has come near and lifted the burden.

The self that receives this gift begins to live differently. The frantic performance slows. The defensive posture softens. The need for recognition loosens its grip, because recognition has already been given by the only One whose recognition ultimately matters. "You are my beloved," the voice speaks over the waters of baptism, and the self that hears this word can finally exhale. The audience of one has rendered its verdict, and the verdict is love.

"The self that has been loved is freed to love. The self that has been held is freed to hold others."

This freedom doesn't withdraw from the world. It enters more deeply. The self that has been loved is freed to love. The self that has been held is freed to hold others. The self that has received an identity no longer needs to defend one, and so can turn outward toward the neighbor, the stranger, the suffering world. The chapters of this book have traced this movement: from diagnosis to invitation, from autosanctity to solidarity, from the exhausted self to the self that rests in Another and rises to serve.

The hegemonospheres will keep forming. The powers will keep competing. The algorithms will keep capturing attention. The culture wars will keep burning. None of this disappears because we've named it. The world remains fractured, and the fractures run deep.

But within the fractures, communities of another kind are possible: communities where identity is received rather than achieved, where belonging doesn't depend on performance, where failure is met with forgiveness rather than exile, where the weary self can lay down its divinity and be, blessedly, creaturely. The church, at its best, has always been such a community. At its worst, it has practiced its own versions of autosanctity with devastating effect. The critique cuts both ways. The invitation extends to all.

The practices matter. The Tech Sabbath that recovers the desert in the digital age. The attention to housing and embodied need that refuses to spiritualize away material suffering. The lament that sits with Job in the ashes and refuses easy answers. The solidarity that crosses every divide to stand with suffering neighbors. The patient formation that shapes people, over years and decades, into those capable of faithful discernment. None of these practices will be featured on platforms optimized for engagement. All of them will be essential to whatever renewal emerges.

140

Hope, in the Christian account, isn't optimism. Optimism is a calculation of probabilities. Hope is a theological virtue: a gift of the Spirit that enables us to live toward a future that isn't yet visible, to act in faith when the evidence is against us, to persist in love when love seems futile. This hope knows that the child born in Bethlehem would grow to be executed by the empire, that the path of incarnate love leads through suffering and death. But it also knows that death didn't have the last word. Resurrection hope is the stubborn conviction that even in death, God is at work bringing life.

So as you close these pages, the invitation remains. You don't have to be your own god. You don't have to construct an identity from scratch. You don't have to perform for an audience that will never be satisfied. You don't have to defend sacred ground that was never meant to bear your weight. You can be held. You can be named. You can be loved into existence by a Love that precedes you and will outlast you.

The sacred self is exhausted. It's been performing for so long. The construction is never complete. The recognition is never enough. At last, there's another way.

The breath came before the algorithm. The Word was spoken before the code was written. And when all the systems have run their course, when the platforms fall silent, and the hegemonospheres crumble, the love that called the cosmos into being will still be singing over creation, making all things new.

Rest isn't elsewhere. It's here:

in the identity you receive,
in the love that holds you,
in the self that learns to say "I'm not my own,"
and finds, at last, the rest it could never give itself.

Bibliography

Allison, Graham. *Destined for War: Can America and China Escape Thucydides's Trap?* Boston: Houghton Mifflin Harcourt, 2017.

Australian Bureau of Statistics. "Estimating Homelessness: Census 2021." Released 22 March 2023. https://www.abs.gov.au/statistics/people/housing and https://www.abs.gov.au/statistics/people/housing/estimating-homelessness-census/2021.

Barth, Karl. *Church Dogmatics* III/2. Translated by G. W. Bromiley et al. Edinburgh: T&T Clark, 1960.

Bass, Dorothy C. *Receiving the Day: Christian Practices for Opening the Gift of Time.* San Francisco: Jossey-Bass, 1999.

Billheimer, P. *Don't Waste Your Sorrows.* CLC, 1993.

Bromiley, G. W. (ed.). "Suffering", in *The International Standard Bible Encyclopedia.* Vol.4. Eerdmans, 1995.

Buolamwini, Joy, and Timnit Gebru. "Gender Shades: Intersectional Accuracy Disparities in Commercial Gender Classification." *Proceedings of Machine Learning Research* 81 (2018): 77–91.

Burton-Christie, Douglas. *The Word in the Desert: Scripture and the Quest for Holiness in Early Christian Monasticism.* Oxford: Oxford University Press, 1994.

Carson, D. A. *How Long Oh Lord.* Baker, 2006.

Center on Budget and Policy Priorities. "Federal Rental Assistance Fact Sheets." Updated 23 January 2025. https://www.cbpp.org/research/housing and https://www.cbpp.org/research/housing/federal-rental-assistance-fact-sheets#US.

Crawford, Matthew B. *The World Beyond Your Head: On Becoming an Individual in an Age of Distraction*. New York: Farrar, Straus and Giroux, 2016.

Economy, Elizabeth C. *The Third Revolution: Xi Jinping and the New Chinese State*. New York: Oxford University Press, 2018.

Gumbel, N. *Searching Issues: Suffering*. Alpha, 2008.

Habel, N. C. "The Book of Job", in *The Old Testament Library*. Westminster, 1985.

Haidt, Jonathan, and Greg Lukianoff. *The Coddling of the American Mind: How Good Intentions and Bad Ideas Are Setting Up a Generation for Failure*. New York: Penguin, 2018.

Hartley, J. E. "The Book of Job", *The New International Commentary on the Old Testament*. Eerdmans, 1988.

Heschel, Abraham Joshua. *The Sabbath: Its Meaning for Modern Man*. New York: Farrar, Straus and Giroux, 1951.

Holland, Tom. *Dominion: How the Christian Revolution Remade the World*. New York: Basic, 2019.

Housing and Development Board, Government of Singapore. "Public Housing: A Singapore Icon." https://www.hdb.gov.sg/about-us/our-role/public-housing-a-singapore-icon.

Kang, David C. *East Asia Before the West: Five Centuries of Trade and Tribute*. New York: Columbia University Press, 2010.

Keller, T. *Walking With God Through Pain and Suffering*. Penguin, 2015.

Kelsey, David. *Eccentric Existence: A Theological Anthropology*. 2 vols. Louisville: Westminster John Knox, 2009.

Kushner, H. S. *When Bad Things Happen to Good People*. Anchor, 2004.

Lanier, Jaron. *Ten Arguments for Deleting Your Social Media Accounts Right Now*. New York: MacMillan, 2018.

Lewis, C. S. *A Grief Observed*. HarperOne, 2001.

Lewis, C. S. *The Problem of Pain*. HarperOne, 2015.

McAlpine, Stephen. "A Sexular Age." stephenmcalpine.com, July 11, 2015. https://stephenmcalpine.com/a-sexular-age/.

McAlpine, Stephen. *Being the Bad Guys: How to Live for Jesus in a World That Says You Shouldn't.* London: The Good Book Company, 2021.

McLuhan, Marshall. *Understanding Media: Extensions of Man.* New York: McGraw-Hill, 1964.

Mearsheimer, John J. *The Tragedy of Great Power Politics.* New York: W. W. Norton, 2001.

Mission Australia. "Response to Report on Government Services 2024: Housing and Homelessness." 21 January 22, 2024. https://www.missionaustralia.com.au/media-centre/media-releases/2024/mission-australias-response-to-report-on-government-services-2024-housing-and-homelessness/.

National Low Income Housing Coalition. *The Gap: A Shortage of Affordable Homes.* Washington: NLIHC, March 2025. https://nlihc.org/gap.

Noble, Safiya Umoja. *Algorithms of Oppression: How Search Engines Reinforce Racism.* New York: NYU Press, 2018.

O'Donovan, Oliver. *The Ways of Judgment.* Grand Rapids: Eerdmans, 2005.

Pontifical Council for Justice and Peace. *Compendium of the Social Doctrine of the Church.* Vatican City: Libreria Editrice Vaticana, 2004. https://www.vatican.va/roman_curia/pontifical_councils/justpeace/documents/rc_pc_justpeace_doc_20060526_compendio-dott-soc_en.html.

Rieff, Philip. *The Triumph of the Therapeutic: Uses of Faith after Freud.* New York: Harper & Row, 1966.

Slaughter, Anne-Marie. *A New World Order.* Princeton: Princeton University Press, 2004.

Smith, James K. A. *Desiring the Kingdom: Worship, Worldview, and Cultural Formation.* Grand Rapids: Baker Academic, 2009.

Smith, James K.A. *How (Not) to Be Secular: Reading Charles Taylor.* Grand Rapids: Eerdmans, 2014.

Taylor, Charles. *A Secular Age.* Cambridge, MA: Harvard University Press, 2007.

Twenge, Jean M. *iGen: Why Today's Super-Connected Kids Are Growing Up Less Rebellious, More Tolerant, Less Happy—and Completely Unprepared for Adulthood.* New York: Atria, 2017.

U.S. Department of Housing and Urban Development. *The 2024 Annual Homeless Assessment Report (AHAR) to Congress, Part 1: Point-in-Time Estimates of Homelessness.* Washington: HUD, December 2024. https://www.huduser.gov/portal/datasets/ahar.html and https://www.huduser.gov/portal/datasets/ahar/2024-ahar-part-1-pit-estimates-of-homelessness-in-the-us.html.

Volf, Miroslav. *Work in the Spirit: Toward a Theology of Work.* Oxford: Oxford University Press, 1991.

Ward, Benedicta, trans. *The Sayings of the Desert Fathers: The Alphabetical Collection.* Collegeville: Cistercian, 1975.

Weil, Simone. *Waiting for God.* Translated by Emma Craufurd. New York: Harper & Row, 1951.

Appendix 1: Discussion Guide

PART I: DIAGNOSING THE SACRED SELF

Autosanctity: The Sacralization of Self in a Supposedly Secular Age

1.   The chapter claims that "the West hasn't abandoned the sacred; it's relocated it." Where do you see evidence of this relocation in your own life, relationships, or institutions?

2.   Autosanctity appears across the political spectrum in different forms: progressive autosanctity centers on identity and recognition, while conservative autosanctity centers on liberty and choice. How have you seen these rival autosanctities clash in your community, and how might recognizing this shared grammar change the conversation?

3.   "There's no sabbath for the autosanct self." What does it feel like to live under the pressure of endless self-construction? Where do you experience this exhaustion most acutely?

4.   The chapter suggests that consent has become the sole remaining moral criterion in autosanct culture. What gets lost when "Is this good?" is replaced by "Is this healthy for me?" and when external moral standards are dismissed as oppression?

5.   What would it mean for you to receive your identity as gift rather than achievement? What practices, relationships, or communities might help you lay down the burden of self-construction?

Tech Sabbath: Recovering the Desert in the Digital Age

1.   The desert fathers and mothers sought God in solitude and silence. The chapter describes our digital environment as the "anti-

desert," filling every gap and colonizing every pause. What inner voices or unfinished business do you avoid through constant connectivity?

2. "We become what we attend to, and attention itself must be trained, protected, and sometimes radically withdrawn." How has your attention been shaped by the platforms you use? What have you become better at noticing, and what have you lost the capacity to see?

3. The chapter describes the monks' confrontation with "demons" in the desert: acedia, vainglory, lust, anger. What inner realities surface when you step away from screens? How might these revelations be gifts rather than threats?

4. What would a Tech Sabbath look like in your life? What fears or resistances arise when you imagine a full day without digital connection?

5. The chapter insists this isn't Luddism but selective, intentional withdrawal. How can communities help one another practice this withdrawal without becoming judgmental or legalistic about technology use?

PART II: AUTOSANCTITY IN PUBLIC LIFE

The Rise of Hegemonospheres: Power Blocs, Patron States, and the New World Disorder

1. The chapter describes hegemonospheres as zones of political, economic, and informational influence dominated by major powers. How does living within a particular hegemonosphere shape what you can see, believe, and imagine?

2. "Every system of concentrated power generates victims." Who are the victims of the hegemonosphere you inhabit, and what would it mean to see them, name them, and stand with them?

3. The chapter suggests that Christians across hegemonospheric divides share a common faith and a common Lord. How can the global church maintain bonds of fellowship across political lines when geopolitical competition pressures toward division?

4. How might autosanctity at the national or civilizational level ("our way of life," "our values") mirror autosanctity at the individual level? What happens when collective identity becomes sacred ground?

5. The prophetic tradition insists that no political arrangement is beyond moral judgment. How can people of faith exercise this prophetic witness toward their own hegemonosphere while living faithfully within it?

Philip Yancey, Celebrity, Brokenness, and Me

1. The chapter describes the "parasocial bond" we form with authors and public figures. What relationships of this kind have shaped your faith, and how does learning of a leader's failure affect those bonds?

2. "Celebrity culture creates platforms that amplify autosanctity while undermining accountability." How do the structures of Christian publishing, speaking circuits, and social media contribute to the conditions that produce spectacular failures?

3. I confess my own complicity in the dynamics I critique. What does it look like to hold the tension between diagnosing cultural problems and acknowledging that we participate in them?

4. The chapter asks what we do with the books and teachings of fallen leaders. How do you navigate the question of whether truth spoken by a hypocrite remains true?

5. What would it look like for the church to build communities where leaders are "truly known by people who have both the access and the authority to intervene"? What structures would need to change?

A Place to Call Home: Why Affordable Housing Demands Church and Society's Urgent Attention

1. The chapter argues that housing insecurity is a spiritual crisis, eroding the conditions necessary for prayer, community, and formation. How have you seen housing precarity affect the faith lives of individuals or families in your context?

2.   "The places where we live shape who we become." What does this claim suggest about the relationship between material conditions and spiritual flourishing? How might autosanctity's focus on inner authenticity blind us to these material realities?

3.   The Hebrew word for "dwell" gives us the word for God's indwelling presence (Shekinah). How might this theological connection reshape how your church thinks about housing ministry?

4.   What assets does your church or community possess (land, buildings, relationships, political voice) that could be deployed toward housing justice? What would need to change to deploy them?

5.   The chapter connects housing to Matthew 25: "Whatever you did for one of the least of these, you did for me." How does this identification of Christ with the homeless challenge the self-focused spirituality of autosanctity?

Sitting with Venezuela

1.   The chapter models holding multiple truths simultaneously: Maduro's regime was a horror, and the intervention raised serious concerns. When have you found it difficult to hold complexity without collapsing into a tribal position?

2.   "Would I feel the same way about this if the partisan valence were reversed?" How do you test yourself for motivated reasoning on political and moral questions? What practices help you see past your own biases?

3.   The chapter refuses to resolve into certainty, ending with "genuinely uncertain." How does autosanctity's demand for identity-confirming positions make this kind of intellectual humility difficult?

4.   The chapter notes that critics and supporters of the intervention might both be inconsistent. How can we move past "your opponents are hypocrites" toward genuine moral reasoning about what is true and good?

149

5.　　What does it look like to "sit with" a difficult situation rather than rushing to judgment? How might this posture be a spiritual discipline in an age of instant takes and algorithmic outrage?

PART III: SUFFERING, TECHNOLOGY, AND THE LIMITS OF THE SELF

No Easy Answers: What Job Reveals About Suffering, Silence, and the God Who Weeps with Us

1.　　Job's friends held to the doctrine of divine retribution: the righteous prosper, the wicked suffer. Where do you see contemporary versions of this theology, including in therapeutic or "manifest your destiny" forms?

2.　　The chapter argues that suffering exposes the inadequacy of the sacred self to bear the weight of ultimate meaning. How have experiences of suffering (your own or others') challenged the assumption that you can construct meaning from within yourself?

3.　　"It's acceptable to question God." How does this permission differ from the way questions are often treated in faith communities? What would it look like for your community to make space for lament and protest?

4.　　The chapter points toward a "crucified God" who suffers with us. How does this image of God differ from the distant, unmoved deity that many people reject? How does it change your experience of suffering?

5.　　"Suffering only makes sense in the light of the final chapter." How does resurrection hope allow you to hold suffering without either minimizing it or being destroyed by it?

The Breath and the Algorithm: A Christian Theological Response to Artificial Intelligence

1.　　The chapter warns against both techno-utopianism and apocalyptic dread, calling both "fundamentally eschatological." Where do you see these narratives operating in conversations about AI, and how does Christian hope offer an alternative?

2.	If human distinctiveness has traditionally been defined by capacities (reason, language, creativity) that machines can now replicate, where does dignity rest? How does grounding the imago Dei in relationship rather than function change the conversation?

3.	"The threat isn't that AI will replace us. The threat is that we'll forget who we are." What does this distinction mean for how we should engage with AI technologies in our work, education, and daily life?

4.	The chapter emphasizes the church's embodied practices (gathering, sharing bread and wine, laying hands, baptizing) as prophetic witness. How do these practices counter the disembodiment that digital technologies encourage?

5.	"The breath came before the algorithm." What does it mean to hold onto this priority as AI becomes more pervasive? How can the church form people for faithful discernment in an age of intelligent machines?

PART IV: THE SELF THAT RESTS

Christmas and the Hope of the World: The Light of Christ That Enters Everything

1.	The chapter claims that the Incarnation is "an ontological claim": something has happened to the very structure of reality. How does this differ from understanding Christmas as merely inspirational or sentimental?

2.	"The hope of Christmas isn't optimism." What is the difference between optimism (a calculation of probabilities) and hope (a theological virtue)? Where in your life do you need hope rather than optimism?

3.	The chapter addresses contemporary crises (ecological collapse, displacement, misinformation, hunger) through the lens of the Incarnation. How does the claim that "God has married Godself to creation permanently" reshape your engagement with these challenges?

4.   The chapter insists that Jesus was Jewish and that Christian antisemitism has been a horror. How does this acknowledgment shape how you read the Christmas story, especially in light of contemporary conflicts in the land where it began?

5.   How does the Incarnation offer an answer to autosanctity's exhaustion? What would it mean to receive the gift of Christmas: an identity given, a worth declared, a burden lifted?

We're One Australian People: A Christian Reflection After Bondi

1.   The chapter was written in immediate response to tragedy. How does faith shape what we say (and don't say) in moments of fresh grief? What does it look like to sit with others in pain without rushing to explanation?

2.   "Standing with the Jewish community isn't optional for those who follow Jesus; it flows from the very logic of our faith." How does this claim challenge Christians to examine their own history and present posture toward Jewish neighbors?

3.   The chapter calls for "grace for each other," including political opponents and leaders who won't get it perfectly right. How does this posture resist the autosanct impulse to defend our tribe and condemn others?

4.   "The attackers wanted to fracture us." How does the choice to remain "one people" become a form of resistance to violence and hatred? What does this solidarity require of you in your own context?

5.   The chapter ends with a liturgical prayer. How can communal prayer and worship form us into the kind of people who respond to tragedy with grief, solidarity, and hope rather than fear, tribalism, and vengeance?

Appendix 2: Would You Help?

Writing a book takes immense effort. It's a sustained labor of love over months, even years. Every page carries hours of thought, prayer, revision, and hope. And while the writing may be solitary, the life of a book is communal. That's where you come in. If this book has meant something to you, I'd be deeply grateful if you could help it find its way into more hands and hearts.

There are two simple but powerful ways you can do that.

First, consider leaving a short review on Amazon (and Goodreads would be wonderful too). Even just a few sentences can help others discover the book, as reviews significantly influence how books are recommended and shared online. You can do that by visiting Amazon or searching for this book and writing a review. Even a short note helps people find the book.

Second, if the book has stirred something in you, would you share it with others: friends, groups, churches, or anyone who might benefit from its message?

Your support helps keep this work going, and it means more than I can say. Thank you for being part of this journey.

Find this book on these pages:

1. Amazon:

https://www.amazon.com.au/stores/author/B008NI4ORQ

2. Goodreads:

https://www.goodreads.com/author/show/20347171.Graham_Joseph _Hill

3. Author Website:

https://grahamjosephhill.com/books/

Appendix 3: About Me

Graham Joseph Hill (OAM, PhD) is an Adjunct Research Fellow and Associate Professor at Charles Sturt University, and one of Australia's most prolific and awarded Christian authors. He's written more than twenty books, including *Salt, Light, and a City*, which was named Jesus Creed's 2012 Book of the Year (church category); *Healing Our Broken Humanity* (with Grace Ji-Sun Kim), named Outreach Magazine's 2019 Resource of the Year (culture category); and *World Christianity*, shortlisted for the 2025 Australian Christian Book of the Year. In 2024, Graham was awarded the Medal of the Order of Australia (OAM) for his service to theological education. He lives in Sydney with his wife, Shyn.

Author and Ministry Websites

GrahamJosephHill.com
GrahamJosephHill.Substack.com
youtube.com/@GrahamJosephHill_Author
Linktr.ee/dailydevotions
facebook.com/grahamjosephhill/
instagram.com/grahamjosephhill/
amazon.com.au/stores/author/B008NI4ORQ
goodreads.com/author/show/20347171.Graham_Joseph_Hill

Books

See all my books at GrahamJosephHill.com/books

Appendix 4: Connect With Me

I'd love to stay connected with you. You can sign up to my Substack, Spirituality and Society with Hilly, where I share new writing, spiritual reflections, and updates on future books. Please find me on Substack: https://grahamjosephhill.substack.com

You can also find my books on my website: https://grahamjosephhill.com/books

You can also connect with me through my Facebook author page: https://www.facebook.com/GrahamJosephHill/